PRAISE FOR *THE STYLE FORMULA*

"Aricia Symes nails the current realities of navigating fashion, especially while balancing the pressure of fast trends and how to approach building a timeless wardrobe. Aricia's passion and technique in understanding style and all the variables that make each person's unique Style ID make this a must read."

—Lucia Budwick
Chief of Staff, Coca-Cola Northeast

"*The Style Formula* is so much more than a 'how-to guide.' Symes cracks the code, taking the emotion and mystery out of dressing with success each day. With proven strategies and science-based facts mixed with tender stories of challenging moments in her own life as well as her clients', Symes shows us anyone can learn to balance their assets with their challenges to find a winning style!"

—Pam Lynch
Former SVP at Tommy Hilfiger and former SVP at Polo Ralph Lauren

"The way we dress and what we wear in public has evolved. In *The Style Formula*, Aricia Symes describes how to understand our body type so we are equipped to navigate our wardrobes with confidence. This book is *the* road map to bespoke personal style!"

—Jill Palese
Senior Fashion Designer, New Balance, Lands' End, Jones New York, Gottex & Founder, Call To Action®

"As a former New England Patriots cheerleader and salon owner, I'm no stranger to juggling multiple roles—from making promotional appearances to working behind the scenes at fashion shows and events. With years of experience both in front of and behind the camera, I know firsthand how challenging it can be to manage teams, balance responsibilities, and maintain a polished look through it all. Aricia Symes's *The Style Formula* is an invaluable resource for expert styling advice, practical outfit ideas, and the overall organization needed to help you look and feel your best in every situation."

—April Lyn Graffeo
Former Patriots Cheerleader, Salon Owner, and Unfoldid client

"Aricia demystifies style, offering a science-backed approach to building a wardrobe that truly reflects your authentic self . . . prepare to unfold your Style ID and dress with newfound confidence and ease."

—**Alisa Marks**
Executive Fashion Editor at Elle UK, Marie Claire UK, and UK Mirabella

THE Style FORMULA

ARICIA SYMES

The Style Formula

THE art AND science OF WHAT TO WEAR

Advantage | Books

Copyright © 2025 by Aricia Symes.

All rights reserved. No part of this book may be used or reproduced in any manner whatsoever without prior written consent of the author, except as provided by the United States of America copyright law.

Published by Advantage Books, Charleston, South Carolina.
An imprint of Advantage Media.

ADVANTAGE is a registered trademark, and the Advantage colophon is a trademark of Advantage Media Group, Inc.

Printed in the United States of America.

10 9 8 7 6 5 4 3 2 1

ISBN: 979-8-89188-029-0 (Paperback)
ISBN: 979-8-89188-030-6 (eBook)

Library of Congress Control Number: 2025903500

Cover design by Analisa Smith.
Layout design by Ruthie Wood.

This publication is designed to provide accurate and authoritative information in regard to the subject matter covered. It is sold with the understanding that the publisher is not engaged in rendering legal, accounting, or other professional services. If legal advice or other expert assistance is required, the services of a competent professional person should be sought.

> Advantage Books is an imprint of Advantage Media Group. Advantage Media helps busy entrepreneurs, CEOs, and leaders write and publish a book to grow their business and become the authority in their field. Advantage authors comprise an exclusive community of industry professionals, idea-makers, and thought leaders. For more information go to **advantagemedia.com**.

To my family who stuck with me through drafts and doubts

CONTENTS

INTRODUCTION 1

PART I 17
A Dressing Mindset

CHAPTER 1 19
A Wardrobe Crisis, Resolved

CHAPTER 2 35
Dressing for You

PART II 51
Discovering Your Style Elements

CHAPTER 3 53
Understanding Your Body's Architecture

CHAPTER 4 71
Modifying Balance Through Cut,
Color, Texture, and More

CHAPTER 5 87
Learning Your Color Science

CHAPTER 6 107
Reflecting Your Likes and Lifestyle

PART III 129
Crafting Your Closet

CHAPTER 7 131
Building Your Foundational Wardrobe

CHAPTER 8 159
How to Build Easy and Creative Outfits

CONCLUSION 185

ACKNOWLEDGMENTS 189

ABOUT THE AUTHOR 191

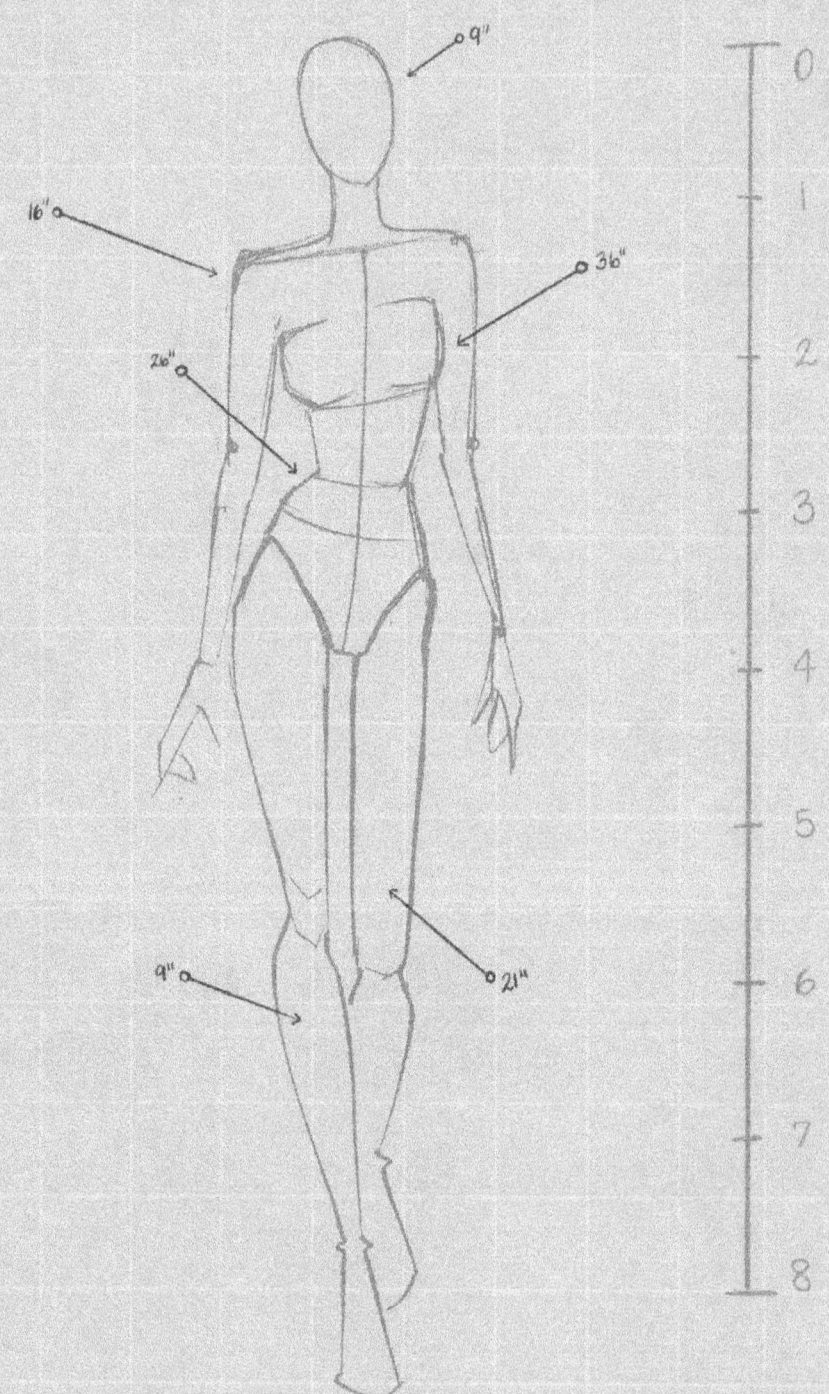

INTRODUCTION

I can still remember the first time a client cried in front of me. She had recently had a baby and was feeling like she didn't know how to dress after all the changes she was experiencing. She booked her appointment and shared that she didn't have a lot to spend on additional appointments or an entirely new wardrobe.

When we met for our first session, she revealed that she was apprehensive about the idea of working with a stylist. The idea of inviting someone to look at her closet and help her figure out how to dress her own body felt discouraging—even a bit silly. "Shouldn't I be able to just figure this out for myself?" she wondered out loud. I quickly assured her that she was not alone in feeling this way.

While there is an oversupply of fashion advice, there is a scarcity of resources to help you build a foundational wardrobe that works for you and your unique body, lifestyle, and preferences. It's no surprise that so many of us can't "just figure it out" for ourselves. And because how we dress is such a big part of how we show up in the world, it is natural to have some form of anxiety about getting it right.

For my client, we addressed that anxiety by focusing first not on her clothes—but on her. We discussed her lifestyle needs and fashion preferences, recorded a few key body measurements, and defined her color palette. With these points in mind, we then went to her closet to identify some items she liked and some that she didn't like, as well as some that she liked but didn't know how to wear. We began to put pieces together, creating looks that complemented her body architecture, coloring, and lifestyle in a way that fit her preferences. Aware that she was budget conscious, I wanted to give her as many choices as possible without going shopping, so we prioritized using pieces she already owned.

As she tried on one outfit, she suddenly got quiet. She stared at herself in the mirror silently, while I felt a nervous knot form in my stomach. Then her eyes started tearing up.

Cue the panic.

"Are you okay?" I asked tentatively, while frantically rummaging for tissues.

The client took a deep breath and then managed to get out: "I just look *so good*."

Cue the sigh of relief.

My client went on to explain how anxious she'd been about the appointment. She talked about the emotional struggles she'd faced dealing with her changing body during and after pregnancy. "I haven't looked or felt this great in ages," she revealed, a smile on her face. "I didn't know I *could* look like this."

Then the two of us did a small happy dance right there in her closet.

Here is the thing: nothing had changed. She was the same person she'd been an hour earlier. She hadn't gotten a facial, or gone on a diet, or dyed her hair, or gotten Botox. The only thing that had changed was the clothes. And they weren't even new clothes. She had *tons* of great items. We had simply put together outfits for her using what she already owned, while avoiding those items in her closet that I knew would not work for her.

So, what was the difference? What happened in the closet in that one hour to make this person come to tears and realize, "Hey, I look great"?

It all came down to science.

The Formula to Unlocking Your Style IDentity

I teach the art and science of style—not only to new moms, but to all people. My clients learn about the Style Formula: a formula for creating looks that work for them and reflect how they want to look. They can then apply it themselves, every time they get dressed.

Much like people want a home they can feel at ease in, they also want clothes they can feel at ease in—while also feeling authentic, confident, and empowered. A house is a functional structure. Your clothes should be functional too. A house becomes a home when you add interior decorating—the rugs, textures, paintings, and knickknacks you love. Say, your grandmother's tablecloth, or your kids' paintings on the fridge. Similarly, your clothes can go beyond function, allowing you to express yourself confidently for any occasion.

I am the founder and lead stylist of Unfoldid, a personal styling company that prioritizes personal well-being. The name Unfoldid stems from the idea that we help you *unfold* your style identity, or your Style ID. The foundation of the Style ID is the Style Formula, which aims to demystify, simplify, and de-stress the act of creating outfits. For each client, my goal is to give them a simple formula that applies to any occasion and helps them present themselves the way they want to be seen. The glimmer of excitement in their eyes when we get it just right is why I do this.

Based on objective elements like body architecture and color science, the formula guides them to understand how each piece of clothing can change the way their body looks to reveal a style that is authentic to them. The true self emerges, unfolds from within, bringing a newfound confidence that empowers. No more guessing and no more second-guessing.

That is my goal for every Unfoldid client—and it is my goal for you.

What began as a one-woman start-up has become a growing company with a full team of stylists. Established in 2010, Unfoldid works with clients throughout the greater Boston area and beyond. Thanks to virtual consultations, we are now collaborating with people across the globe. We offer personal shopping, wardrobe consultation, body architecture education, and closet-editing services.

We have worked with individuals and companies including Boston Consulting Group, Tripadvisor, and Facebook—to name just a few—to help their employees learn the art and science of style. We've supported politicians, on-air personalities, and more. We've worked with everyone from stay-at-home moms to people preparing for the Grammys red carpet.

Across the board, whether I've been working with high-powered attorneys or students preparing for their first job interviews, I've seen one thing again and again: there is a lot of confusion around getting dressed—more specifically, getting dressed in a way that makes us feel *good*.

When you take a closer look at the context, it's no wonder we feel this way. Outside influences tend to make things hard. Celebrities, social media, and the fashion industry tell us what's cool and encourage us to buy more to try and keep up. Plus, with smartphones everywhere, and people taking photos and recording videos, it can feel like there's pressure to look amazing and photo-ready at all times.

What if you could quiet all those external influences and find a way to dress *for yourself* that suits *your* body, *your* complexion, *your* lifestyle, and *your* taste? What if you had a closet of clothes where you could confidently pick any piece, throw it on, and feel great? What if you could put together the perfect outfit for any event—in ten minutes or less—and confidently head out the door?

Ahhh ... I can hear the sigh of relief. Your sigh of relief is what we're after—and, for a few of you, perhaps even tears of joy or a happy dance.

In the pages to come, we will deconstruct the components of the Style Formula and show you how to use it to build a wardrobe that will make it easy for you to put together the outfits that will serve you well in *your* life. Not the life of the person you see on social media. Not the life of the celebrity on the red carpet. Your unique life and all that it holds, from first dates to playdates, after-work cocktails, cozy days at home, and beyond.

At the end of each chapter, you'll find an exercise that takes you to your closet to complete a simple task or two that will help you learn more about your Style ID. Your Style ID unlocks a clear understanding of how to create a wardrobe of outfits you love and is created using the Style Formula, which breaks down like this:

The Style Formula

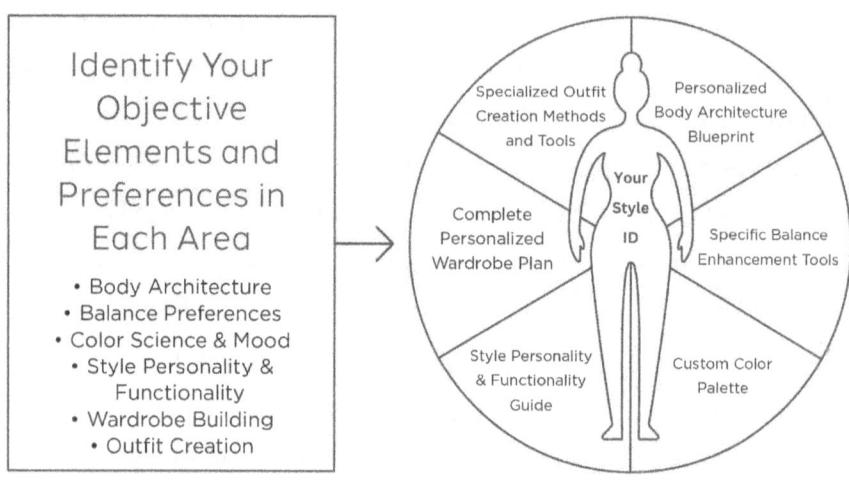

A look at the components that make up the Style Formula

Using the Style Formula, we create your Style ID—giving you a simple, effective system for expressing and elevating your personal style. Each element of your Style ID helps you understand the impact of your clothing choices, equipping you with the knowledge and confidence to select pieces that make you feel effortlessly good.

You can then shop with intention, build a wardrobe that serves you well, and easily put together outfits you love to wear, again and again. You'll objectively understand what works for you and what doesn't and, more importantly, why. That confidence will make creating outfits that much easier—and that much more fun.

Remember playing dress-up as a kid and how fun it was? You didn't look at yourself in the mirror and think, "Does this tutu work for me?" or "Hmm, can I pull off this plastic tiara with the pearls I borrowed from Mom?" You just thought, "I look great." And you were eager to try on the next thing. With this new understanding of how and why clothes work, you can approach dressing today with the same enthusiasm and creativity of your childhood. Wouldn't it be nice to recapture that relationship with clothing? That's what we're here to do.

There Is a Science to Creating Outfits You Love—And You Can Learn It

I love being a stylist. However, I didn't set off to be a stylist from day one. Like most people, it took some time for me to find my professional calling. This was a natural progression for me, but a very surprising transformation to my family and childhood friends. They knew me not as a "fashionista," but as a three-sport athlete who spent most of her days working alongside her four brothers, grubbing around in the garden and tending to the family livestock.

My first official foray into the fashion space started after college, when I put my degrees in international business and Asian studies to use working for an international shoe company. The company had offices in Taiwan, Hong Kong, and the United States. As the operations coordinator, I had plenty of exposure to the design side of the business—inspecting the leather goods used for production, working in the sample room, and liaising with department store chains. I saw firsthand how trends move through the consumer cycle. When the popular style of pant legs changed, we had to design new shoes to work with them; when dresses were in, we needed more heels in the store; and, as different colors trended, we had to design shoes to work with them.

My job with that international shoe company was my entry point into the fashion world—and I *still* use this as an excuse for my extensive shoe collection. You could say I got my foot in the door. It also gave me the opportunity to work overseas, where I was exposed to different cultures and fashions, another pivotal learning experience.

I went on to get my MBA from New York University's Stern School of Business. That led to a string of roles in management and consulting. Again, even though I wasn't actively seeking roles in fashion, that was the direction my career trended. I moved to Europe and spent some time as a consultant at Ernst & Young, where my work included formulating strategy for a textile wholesaler and doing customer segmentation for a chain of apparel stores.

When I was ready to take the next step in my career, I wanted to find something more creative and fulfilling than the business side of fashion. Styling clients checked all the boxes. It allowed me to find balance between my family life and work, and gave me the chance to connect with others and introduce them to the art and science of getting dressed. I liked the idea of styling everyone, not just celebrities. I've always believed that anybody can benefit from understanding how to dress in a way that works for them and expresses who they are. They don't have to be walking the red carpet.

I learned the ins and outs of styling and coloring from Paula Slattery, an expert on the topic, and a consultant on the original *Color Me Beautiful* book. Then, I went to New York and learned all I could about the craft from an established stylist, Stacy London. You may know her from shows like *What Not to Wear*, *Fashionably Late with Stacy London*, or *Wear Whatever the F You Want*. When I completed Stacy's program, she signed a copy of her book for me, with the words: "Aricia! You know your shit." She remains an inspiration.

Using what I'd learned from these experts and through my own research, I started to develop the objective components of the Style Formula and how they shape each person's unique Style ID. I then started sharing what I'd learned with clients, refining my technique in the process.

I learned it all from scratch—and you can too. If you wanted to learn accounting, how to cook, or to speak a language, you might watch a YouTube video, read a book, or take a course. Why should learning how to effectively style yourself be any different? It's a teachable skill.

We talk about the "magic" jeans that make our butts look great or the "magic" first-date outfit that always leads to a second date. These are the clothes that make us feel our best. When we have them on, we feel like we can conquer the world—or conquer the date or the job interview or whatever the occasion may be. But it's not magic, and it's not luck either. It's a formula based on art and science. You like these jeans or that dress because they make your body look the way you want it to look. The result? You feel amazing. That's the power of the Style Formula.

Knowledge Is Power: Understanding What Works and Why

As my business expanded and I began working with more clients, including many powerful and successful people, I often heard that getting dressed in the morning was a uniquely stressful part of their day. Perhaps you can relate to the high of finally finding the perfect pair of jeans, followed by the low of not understanding why those jeans "worked," when so many others did not. When discovering a good pair of jeans seems like luck—or even a miracle—it's easy to see how one can get stuck and want to stop trying. Read on to become unstuck.

It's not surprising that many of my clients experience similar challenges in their closets. I have seen patterns emerge over time. For instance, I often notice people struggling to incorporate a single article of clothing into their outfits; it will just sit in their closet, loved but unworn. They don't realize why they were struggling to make it work—but there is almost always an objective reason for it. For example, it might be that the color or pattern of that item of clothing highlights a particular area of their body.

On the other side of the equation, people may struggle to realize why something does work. When I ask new clients to show me a favorite piece of clothing they have, they can easily reach for a dress or shirt or pair of jeans they love. But they can't articulate why it works for them. They just love the way it makes them feel. Since I've already used the Style Formula to create their Style ID—breaking down their body architecture, coloring, and other elements—I can tell them exactly why. Their favorite dress aligns with their Style ID. It has a fitting neckline, it hits at the right place at the knee, it comes in at the waist and graduates out, it's a complementary color, and so on.

Here's the wonderful thing: once we deconstruct the why of a piece of clothing—why is it so great?—we're able to repeat it. I'm not saying to go out and buy the exact same dress. I'm saying maybe you buy a sweater with the same neckline. Maybe you buy a skirt that also comes in at the waist and graduates out. Once you understand your Style ID, you'll know what traits to look for in clothes. That's how you build a wardrobe of pieces you love.

So many people struggle with "what to wear." Men, women, and nonbinary individuals of all ages, in all kinds of careers, with all kinds of tastes, deal with the clothing conundrum. I've seen teachers wonder what to wear to the first day of school, as if they were kids again. I've seen politicians discuss ad nauseam, often in a group huddle with their staffers, if their outfit communicates the right mixture of affability and power. And I've seen a lot of everyday people worry about what to wear—to work, a wedding, a date, a family reunion, a christening, a funeral …

Whatever your struggle may be, know that you're not alone and there is a solution. There are a lot of fashion "rules" that are complicating matters for all of us, which we'll talk about. And the flurry of fashion advice from well-intentioned blogs, influencers, and magazines can make it all the more complicated, because that advice isn't tailored to your unique needs. The good news: it's solvable. All you need is the knowledge.

Take Time to Learn the Science Now to Save Time Later

Throughout my styling career, I've also met people who have retreated from it all. Feeling frustrated, lacking time, missing guidance—they decide to shove style into the back of the closet of their lives. I get it. I have three kids and got my MBA while starting a family and a new business. At times, clothing may seem like a low priority compared to life's other duties and dreams.

These people might say, "Well, I'm the CEO of a successful company. Why does what I wear matter?" or "I'm a great mom. Why does how I look matter?" or "I've got a PhD. Why would I care what someone says about my outfit? It's who I am on the inside, my brain and spirit, that matters."

These are all true and valid points. However, the reality is that clothing plays a big part in perception. How you dress can impact how you feel and perceive yourself. It can also impact how others perceive you. In fact, research shows that 55 percent of first impressions are made by what we see.[1] People will even make a first impression of you based

---

1   Jackie Rakers, IOM, PFMM, "What Makes a Good First Impression," IOM Blog, March 2016, https://institute.uschamber.com/what-makes-a-good-first-impression/.

on your Zoom background.[2] And those first impressions can be lasting and robust, touching on everything from trustworthiness to competence.

As kids, we may be told not to judge a book by its cover; it isn't quite that simple. There is a reason that people stress about what to wear to a job interview—we know, on some level, we are being judged on our appearance, not just our résumé. I'm not saying that's wrong or right. I'm just saying that it is.

What's more, our society is becoming ever more visual. We have video calls for work and camera phones in our pockets. In that context, the importance of presentation has become more significant. People don't just dress for success in a standard navy suit like they might have in the past; these days, people dress according to their "personal brand." Clothing is a type of visual messaging. When you step into the room, it's one of the first things people notice about you. I want to empower you to have control over the message you're sending.

So taking some time to learn the science for yourself is, in my opinion, a worthy endeavor. Yes, my opinion is biased; after all, I'm a stylist. However, I do truly think that the Style Formula can help anyone dress well without the headaches. Once you've mastered it, you'll be able to identify the *why* of your favorite clothing, which is going to make building a wardrobe and creating great outfits a whole lot easier.

How Art and Science Can Help You Be Objective

With body architecture, color science, and the other elements of the Style Formula supporting your clothing choices, you'll be able to:

---

[2] Abi Cook, Meg Thompson, and Paddy Ross, "Virtual First Impressions: Zoom Backgrounds Affect Judgements of Trust and Competence," *PLoS One* 18, no. 9 (September 2023): e0291444, DOI: https://doi.org/10.1371/journal.pone.0291444.

- Select clothes that highlight or downplay areas with intention and ease.

- Build a functional wardrobe of versatile pieces that work for your body and lifestyle.

- Mix and match your wardrobe effortlessly to create outfits for any occasion, from casual to formal.

- Create a solid foundation for your personal style, empowering you to explore and create confidently.

- Step out each day feeling confident and authentic, knowing your look is a true reflection of who you are.

- Save time and avoid stress with an organized, well-curated wardrobe that works cohesively.

- Develop and refine your style, embracing evolving trends while staying grounded in a look that's uniquely yours.

Maybe you're fed up with getting dressed in the morning. One in three clients of mine shares exactly that attitude. They are exhausted. I'll tell you what I tell them: "The whole point of this endeavor is to take it off your plate." Investing a little bit of time now can save you a lot of time and frustration later, making dressing well something you won't even have to think about—unless you want to.

This Is Not a Rule Book of "Dos and Don'ts"

This is not a book about fashion. It's a book for anyone who wants to make getting dressed effortless. If you are a fashionista, you will still find value here—learning the Style Formula can help you master all those trends and couture moments you love to look at but maybe don't quite know what to do with. But you don't have to be a fashion enthusiast to benefit from this book. It's meant for everyone.

I prefer to avoid rigid "do's" and "don'ts" when it comes to styling. I am not here to tell you that you can never wear crop tops or leopard print or wide-legged jeans or whatever it is that calls to you. I am not here to monitor your taste because taste is completely subjective and wonderfully unique, and everyone has their own. My aim is to help you understand the objective science of it all so that you can then enjoy and play with the more creative side of styling and dressing. Once you understand the Style Formula, you can use it to communicate what you want and enjoy that process of self-expression.

Knowing what works for you doesn't have to be limiting. On the contrary, once you understand the various components of your Style ID, you'll find that things start to fall into place. You'll discover that your options aren't restricted; rather, as you come to understand your personal style, you'll find that your options become much greater. As you comprehend the science side of style, it will allow you to embrace the creative, expressive side more easily. By combining the science and the art, you'll develop a look that not only works for you but also is one that you love.

This book aims to give you a foundational understanding of each component of the Style Formula, and how to use it to create a Style ID. The Style Formula takes a holistic approach that considers the unique characteristics that define you. Each of these elements works together to make up your Style ID. Because personal style is a combination of all these unique elements, you can't focus solely on body architecture or only play with color. The Style ID takes into account everything that makes a person unique, offering a holistic approach and a comprehensive view of your personal style.

In the next chapter, we're going to look at some of the outside influences we face that make getting dressed confusing. Understanding those influences, both internal and external, can help us see how subjective those influences are. The subsequent chapters will cover every component of the Style Formula, including:

- Understanding your body's architecture
- Modifying balance through cut, color, texture, and more
- Learning your color science
- Reflecting your likes and lifestyle, as well as your environment
- Building a wardrobe that works for you
- Confidently crafting outfits that express your individuality

Key points you can expect to learn in this book

As you gain an understanding of the Style Formula and learn to apply it to your life, you will be able to style yourself with ease and step out the door with confidence. No more closet full of unworn clothing items you aren't sure what to do with. No more individual items that don't go with anything else. No more fashion disasters. Just a wardrobe full of pieces that you know how to put together confidently—and that you feel amazing in, because they reflect the true you.

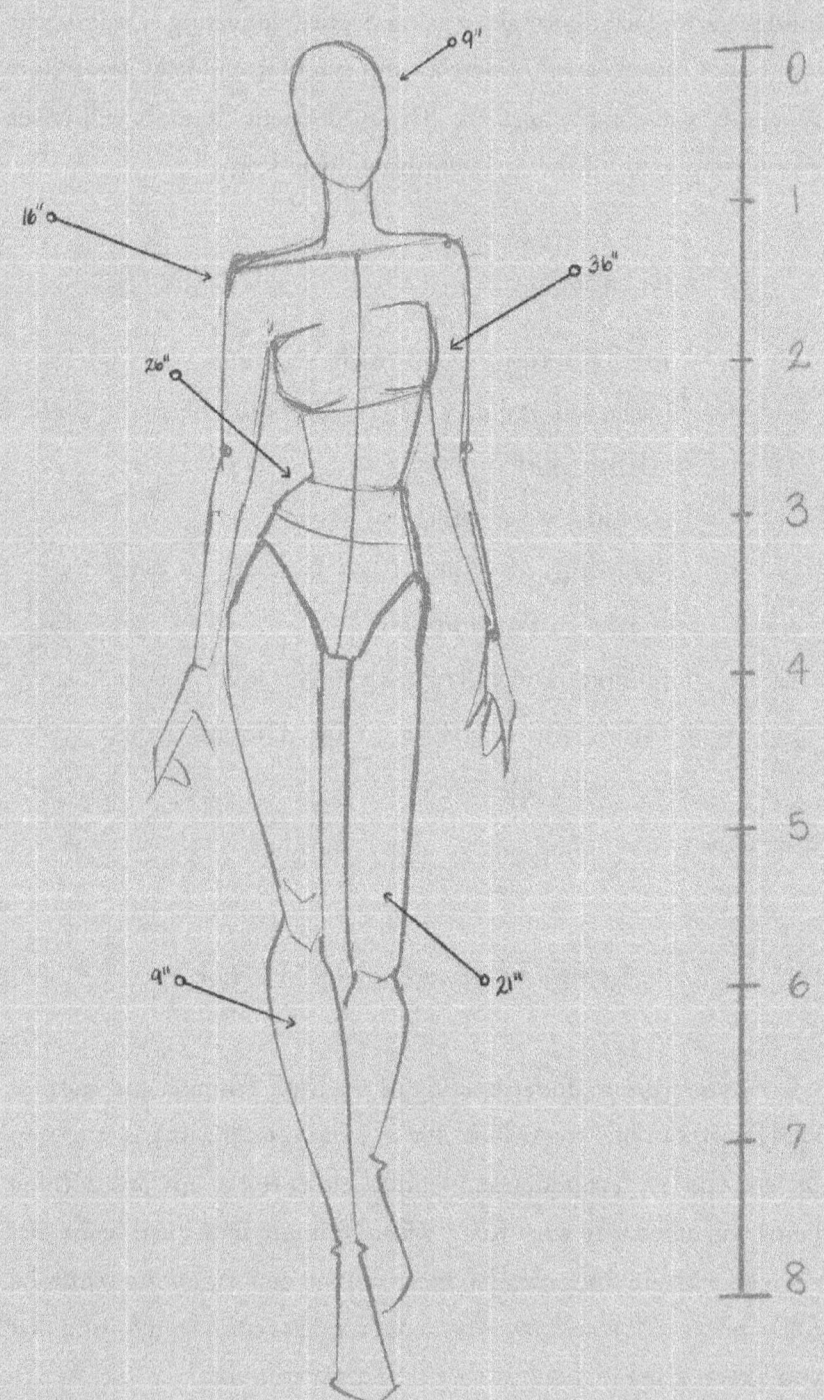

PART I
A Dressing Mindset

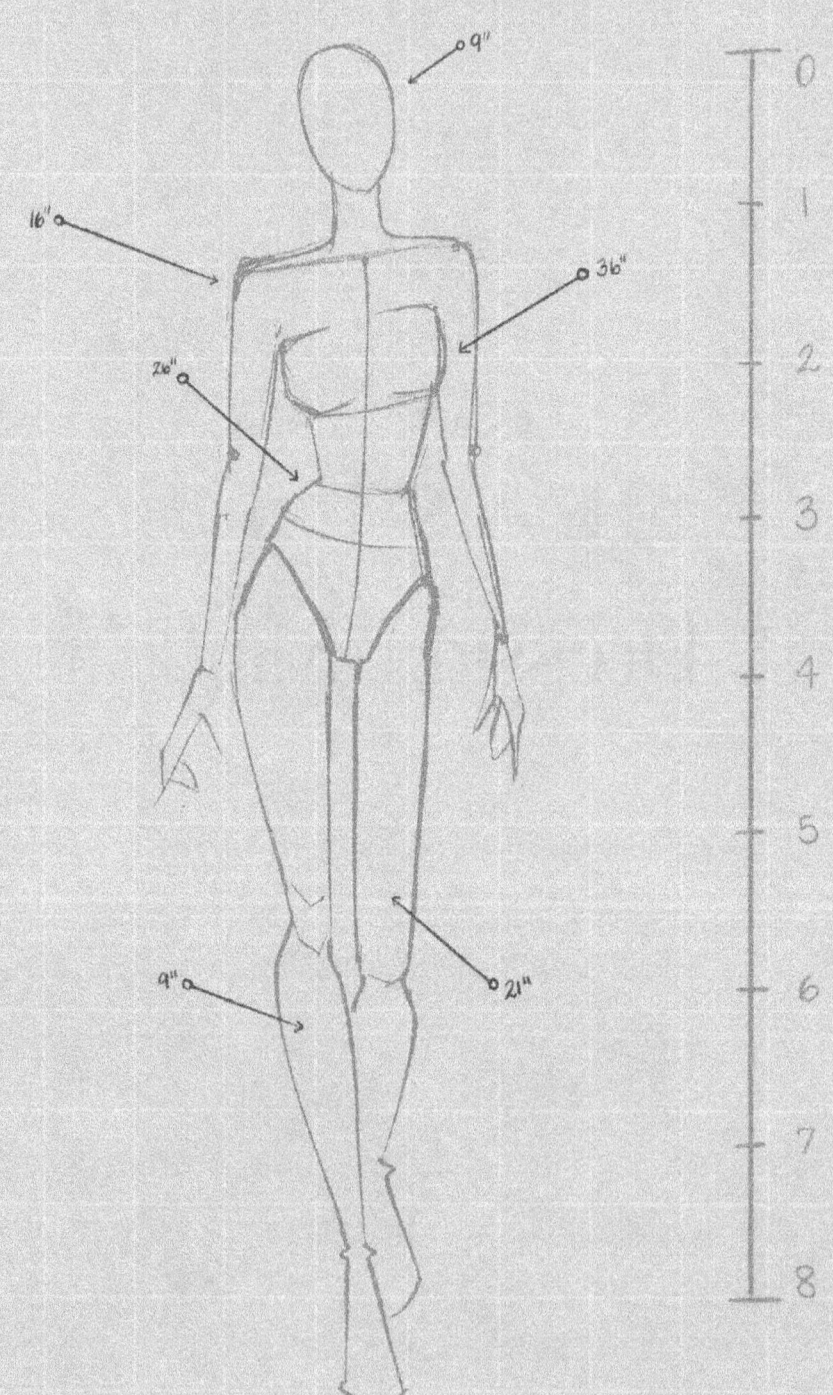

CHAPTER 1

A Wardrobe Crisis, Resolved

One of the most common discussions I have with clients is what I call "the Jeans Talk." Denim is a wardrobe staple. We all have at least one pair of jeans lingering in our closet. Some of us have five or ten pairs. Some have forty.

The Jeans Talk goes something like this: We enter my client's closet, and she shows me her favorite pair of jeans and says, "I love these, because they make my butt look great." They then put on a different pair of jeans—and suddenly, it's "Ugh, my butt looks horrible in these jeans."

Notice how when the jeans look good on us, we attribute it to the jeans—but when we think they look "bad" on us, we blame our own bodies? It's a misconception that I see again and again with clients, and not just with denim. When we like the way we look in an outfit, we attribute it to that outfit, as if clothes can work magic. When we don't like the way we look, it's on us—not the clothes—when, in fact, it really is about the clothes.

This mythology of the magic article of clothing is so prevalent, Hollywood devoted an entire movie to it. *The Sisterhood of the Traveling*

Pants is all about a pair of jeans that looks so good on every member of a young group of girlfriends, they decide to share the jeans.

When I train stylists, I emphasize the importance of giving their client, not the clothes, the control in the conversation. We ask the client how they want to look and empower them to choose the clothes to achieve that look. This starts with understanding their unique body while also understanding that if something doesn't "look good," it's not because of their body; it's because of the article of clothing not being the right cut, length, texture, color, or whatever the case may be.

All that said, I understand the mythology of clothing is really hard to avoid. It's in social media, celebrity culture, the consumer-driven industries of fashion and beauty—even comments we get from friends, mothers, and partners. We'll look at some of those external influences that swirl around all of us in chapter 2. For now, I want to focus on debunking some of the myths we carry with us internally. Because while you can't change the world around you, you can change your understanding of it—and once you see how subjective the mythology of clothing is, you can reshape your relationship to getting dressed and understand it all in a more objective way.

It's Not You; It's the Clothes

Have you ever seen something in a store that looks amazing on the hanger or the mannequin? You grab it in your size and rush to the dressing room to try it on. You slip it on, take a deep breath, look in the mirror, and—disappointment. This is *not* what you were expecting. Why does it look good on the hanger but not on *you*?

Here's the thing: it's not you. There is nothing wrong with you or your body. It's the clothes. You have a pair of jeans or a favorite dress that you know looks great on you—so you know the pieces are out there. It's just that *this* piece is not the right one. You don't have to change your body or your haircut or the color of your eyes. All you have to do is change the clothes. That doesn't mean you have to buy all new clothes; it's more about understanding how to make what you have work for you. A lot of it comes down to understanding balance and proportions, and how cut, color, and texture can be used to adjust balance and proportions.

Before meeting me, many of my clients will read an article or blog about one component of styling—say, color—and assume this is all they need to know. They'll then wonder why implementing that one component does not work. In fact, you need all the components.

I had a client who came to me feeling frustrated, convinced her hips were "too wide." She had already done some online research and found styling tips to downplay her hips, but the results left her feeling even more out of balance. The issue was that her shoulders were actually broader than her hips, so focusing solely on minimizing her hips threw her whole silhouette off. Rather than fixing the problem, it led to even more confusion and frustration.

My role was to help her see that the real solution was in understanding her unique proportions. When she realized that her broader shoulders could actually work to complement her hips, it all started to make sense. I showed her how to use science to reach her unique goals—doing the opposite of the advice she'd found online. Instead of minimizing her hips, we focused on balancing her silhouette by downplaying her shoulders, creating a harmonious look she truly loved.

I had another client who was petite and "dressed tall" by wearing high heels, constantly. Heels are great, and I love a heel some days—but day in and day out, it can be a lot. I showed her that heels didn't have to be the only answer. There are other ways to elongate a silhouette, for example pairing shorter tops with high-waisted bottoms. Another option is dressing in tonal combinations—color schemes made up of various shades of the same hue—from head to toe. Say, light-blue denim and a royal-blue top. This keeps the viewer's eye moving up and down the entire figure. Even accessories can help; a long pendant necklace adds a vertical element that lengthens. The impact of these changes can add just as much visual height as a pair of sky-high stilettos.

It's all about understanding the balance and proportions of your unique body and then applying the right tools to work toward your style goals. And the goal for everyone may not be perfect balance or equilibrium. Some people like to accentuate the upper body while others prefer creating a curvier bottom. You can adapt balance and proportions to any goal—but it requires a holistic approach. Proportions and balance play off each other and relate to your body architecture. Simply changing one part of a picture doesn't necessarily change the entire image. Like my client who wanted to "dress taller," it's usually a combination of things that results in portraying the picture you want.

Balance and proportions are impacted by cut, color, texture, and more. We will address those components in the pages to come. When you understand how those elements work across your body, you will be able to create looks that work for you. Just as importantly, you'll be doing it in an objective way, which helps eliminate the subjective negativity some of us bring to the dressing room—a notoriously emotional place. Dressing rooms are actually *intended* to be emotional spaces—there's been research on how they influence our emotions with their lighting, furniture, and other features.[3] Such features may be engineered to compel you to make impulsive or emotional purchases.

---

[3] Jennifer Hengevelt, "Dressing Rooms: Love It or Leave It! To What Extent Does the Setting of a Dressing Room Influence Consumer Experiences?" University of Twente Student Thesis, 2014, https://essay.utwente.nl/65017/.

Objectivity creates space for us to explore what it is that we really want to convey with our clothes. And the changes don't have to be drastic. One study into menswear suggests that even "minor modifications to clothing styles can impact the information conveyed to perceivers."[4] I am not suggesting you need a wardrobe overhaul. It could be some simple changes in your clothing choices or in the way you work with what you already own.

Debunking the Myths

Maybe you've had those moments. You're getting dressed for a special event and don't have anything that works. Or you're having a tough time getting ready for work in the morning because you prefer a more casual style, and professional clothes feel soul crushing. Or nothing seems to be just right, so you change again, and again, and again, and again.... All the while, there are other things you should or could be doing—like calling your mom or getting the kids on the bus or prepping for that morning meeting.

You aren't alone. I have so many clients who go through this. Some of them resort to "uniform dressing," simply putting on the exact same style of trousers and shirt in different colors. Often, my clients will share their reasons for why they believe they are struggling with their style. I've unpacked some of the most common misconceptions below. Maybe some of these will resonate with you.

---

4   Neil Howlett, Ismail Orakçioğlu, Karen Pine, and Ben C. Fletcher, "The Influence of Clothing on First Impressions: Rapid and Positive Responses to Minor Changes in Male Attire," *Journal of Fashion Marketing and Management* 17 (February 2013): 38-48, DOI: https://doi.org/10.1108/13612021311305128.

MYTH: "I DON'T HAVE THE TIME."

Reality: Taking the time to learn your Style ID now will save you time shopping and getting dressed later.

When we shop without really knowing what works for us, it can be very time consuming. We end up trying on so many pieces that often, after an exhausting try-on session, we find ourselves compromising and coming home with the "best pair I tried today" instead of "the best pair for me." Having too many of these almost-right pieces in your closet can be frustrating when you later try to wear them.

Once you understand details like your silhouette, proportions, and coloring, and you know your Style ID, shopping becomes faster and more focused. You know what you need and what works for your body, lifestyle, needs, and preferences. Imagine if every item in your closet worked like your favorite pair of jeans, and that you already owned all the pieces you need to get dressed. Making outfits would be fast and easy.

MYTH: "I DON'T HAVE THE SPACE IN MY CLOSET."

Reality: By stocking your closet with pieces that work for you and cutting those that don't, you'll save space.

It can be easy to think that more clothing means more outfits. But if you have a cluttered, overcrowded wardrobe, selecting outfits can be overwhelming. Plus, making space for new essentials becomes tricky. In reality, it's all about having the *right* pieces, not more pieces. One perfect pair of black pants is better than ten almost perfect pairs. From both a time and space perspective, I recommend my clients prioritize one-and-done articles of clothing—meaning the article works on its own, with no accessories or gimmicks needed. You paid for this piece of clothing; it should be working for you. You shouldn't be working to make it work.

Many of my clients have clothing that requires work. They'll say, "Well, these jeans are a bit short, so I only wear them with these taller boots," or "This top only works with this belt." That is an inefficient way to build a wardrobe and hinders your ability to get dressed simply. Consider if you go on a work trip and bring those jeans—now you have to bring those boots, just to make that one pair of jeans work. If you bring that top, you have to bring that belt, just to make that one top work. You'll save space in your closet and your suitcase by replacing inefficient pieces like these with pieces that truly work.

MYTH: "I DON'T HAVE THE MONEY."

Reality: When you invest in the right pieces that fit your Style ID, you'll have a better cost-per-wear (CPW), avoid shopping mistakes, and save money.

Knowing your Style ID gives you a clear understanding of how to best spend your clothing dollars, allowing you to invest in what works for you. That could mean a splurge piece or spending more on an anchor piece of clothing that you will incorporate in many different outfits, for example. Think of that almost-perfect pair of black pants—would you rather have three "almost-perfect" pairs at thirty dollars each, or one perfect pair you love at ninety dollars?

Even if you don't have a lot of money to invest now, applying the Style Formula can help you to build a wardrobe over time by spending smarter, not spending more. Over time, you will build a wardrobe that has everything you need—no more last-minute shopping. I think we all have items that we spend a lot of money on that we know aren't quite right. Maybe it's not cut right for us or doesn't match anything else in our closet—or maybe we didn't spend enough on a favorite piece, and it is now worn and needs replacing. Each less-than-perfect purchase is money that we could have spent on something truly special that enhances our wardrobe. There are clothing dollars hanging unworn in all of our closets, likely some with tags still on. With your Style ID guiding you, you can spend your clothing dollars more effectively.

MYTH: "IT'S TOO COMPLICATED."

Reality: The Style Formula silences the noise of external influences when picking clothes and building outfits. Learn it once and you can apply it for the rest of your life.

There is an overabundance of information about style out there, which can be confusing, but building a wardrobe that works is a learnable skill. And you only need to learn your Style ID once. Unless you're planning to become a professional stylist, you can forget about all the other body silhouettes and color types and lifestyles and purposes that shape someone else's Style ID. You only have to focus on you.

Once you understand the Style Formula, there will be so much more clarity about what to buy and how to wear it. The science justifies the truth. Say you have your favorite shirt. You love it; it looks great on you. That's the truth. But *why*? The Style Formula will explain the logic behind it—yes, that shirt looks great on you and *this is why*.

MYTH: "I DON'T LOOK GOOD IN THE CURRENT TRENDS."

Reality: Your Style ID lets you adapt trends to your preferences (or skip them altogether).

When a new trend hits, like a bold color or a fresh style of blazer, it's easy to feel the pull to join in. I often have clients say, "I love bright colors, and they look great on me, but muted hues are everywhere."

Others might tell me, "Everyone is wearing animal prints, but they feel a bit too bold for me."

First, please do not feel obligated to follow trends. Remember, they are fleeting. That said, there are ways that you can incorporate trends effectively into your look, and they can be a great tool to keep your look current—once you understand the basics of your Style ID. In fact, once you've mastered the art and science, there's no trend you can't wear, because you will know how to adapt the trend to your body and lifestyle.

MYTH: "I WILL LOOK TOO [OLD/YOUNG/SERIOUS/CUTE/FLASHY/TRASHY]."

Reality: Your Style ID allows you to confidently present yourself as you perceive yourself. Not "too" anything.

Even if we want to say that appearances don't matter, we know better. We dress up for dates, job interviews, and special events because we know they matter. Most of us are concerned with the visual message we send the world. We want to present ourselves in a certain way (whether consciously or subconsciously), and we may have some fear about sending the wrong message or it being misinterpreted. We wear our fear on our sleeve, so to speak.

I have a lot of clients that use the "too" phrases. "Too old," "too young," "too serious," "too much." Maybe you have a "too" of your own that causes you anxiety. However, at the end of the day, it's not what you wear but how you wear it. That's where your Style Formula comes into play. It can help us master our own visual messaging.

Once we understand how to create the look we want, that makes us feel comfortable and empowered, any fears of being "too" anything dissipate. That confidence can serve us well in all kinds of scenarios, from special events to job interviews. Elizabeth Hart of Tailored for Success, Inc., can attest to what a difference that confidence makes for people.

A Testament to the Power of Styling: Elizabeth Hart, Executive Director, Tailored for Success, Inc.

Tailored for Success empowers job seekers to become economically self-sufficient by providing resources, skills training, and supportive reinforcement. The organization works with clients throughout the greater Boston area, many of whom come from domestic violence or homeless shelters and/or job training or reentry programs. I met Liz, the founder and executive director of Tailored for Success, at RSM Consulting in Boston, where I was hired to speak about building a work wardrobe and dressing for the workplace. Liz was there to do a clothing drive as part of the event. I was inspired by Liz's work and thought there might be ways Unfoldid could help. Giving back is important to us, and we're always looking to make a positive impact by partnering with like-minded organizations.

I met Aricia when we were both invited to speak at an event hosted by a company holding a clothing drive for Tailored for Success. I spoke first to give the participants an idea of what Tailored for Success does, and to highlight the importance of their donations, where their donations were going to go, and so on. Aricia spoke after me, and her presentation was all about putting together professional outfits. Listening to her, I learned a lot about the details of professional dressing—like dressing for a client-facing role versus non-client-facing role. She knew her stuff, and I remember being impressed by her expertise.

After her presentation, Aricia and I started chatting, and she revealed that one of her stylists had always wanted to work with low-income women trying to get back into the workforce. "Do you have any volunteer opportunities?" she asked. Of course, I said yes! Aricia then introduced me to her senior stylist, Amanda, who volunteered to devote one day every week working with Tailored for Success's clients and has continued to volunteer for over a year.

The impact of styling on our clients is immeasurable. Amanda does not just dress our clients. She takes the time to get to know them, asking about everything from their style likes and dislikes to what kind of job they're interviewing for. She also provides education, helping them understand details like the colors and cuts that will work best for them. When she sends me photos of outfits she's put together for her clients, I'm always impressed by what she pulls together. It's a testament to the value of styling.

Early on, it was clear to me how passionate Aricia and her team are about what they do. The Tailored for Success Career Closets—we have one in Cambridge and one in Woburn—are designed to look like boutiques, because we want people to feel like they're visiting a shop, not a nonprofit. Upon Aricia's first visit to the Closet, she recommended that our clothing hangers could use an update. So Aricia and Amanda came in and replaced (at Aricia's cost) hundreds of our old plastic hangers with beautiful black velvet ones, which totally revamped the look of our "closet"! Aricia has such attention to detail, which requires a lot of care and has been a big part of the reason the partnership between Unfoldid and Tailored for Success has been so successful.

When you think about how emotional the struggle of "what to wear" is, that most people have—someone with a limited income has their struggle compounded by financial worries. Clothes aren't a priority when you are worrying about how to pay rent or take care of your children or put food on the table. When women or men are going for an interview, not having the right clothing can be detrimental to their confidence. Imagine sitting in a waiting room for a job interview, alongside other candidates, and worrying that your clothes are not professional enough or somehow indicate that you "don't belong." That adds a whole new level of stress to interviewing, which is already challenging.

When a person has professional clothing on—it doesn't have to be designer, just something nice that fits them—they're going to sit a little bit straighter and they're going to feel more confident. Then they will feel equipped to do the job they're interviewing for, no matter their background. Clothing can be a great equalizer in that way! No matter what your economic situation, being able to tap into the value of styling—to project yourself to the world in the way you want to—is a big thing. That's what Aricia and her team help people do. I am forever grateful to Aricia for her support of Tailored for Success, Inc.

Your Emotions Are Subjective—Science Is Not

Every client is unique, and every person has their own worries—often relating not only to appearances but also to lifestyle. A lot of moms struggle with a desire to be stylish yet functional, for instance. They need a practical outfit that they can basically hose down after a day on the playground with their toddlers. It can't be a dry-clean-only blazer.

News anchors are another great example—and their concerns are very different. They need clothes that they can wear on-air that don't just look good on them but also look good on camera—and that they can afford and wear over and over. That's a whole different ball game that demands other considerations, from lighting to makeup and camera frames. On-screen personalities are very judicious about picking certain colors, for example, taking into account not only their personal color palette but also the technicalities of being on-air.

The Style Formula is similarly technical. Again, it's logical and objective, not subjective, which means it removes the emotionality from the equation. That doesn't mean we're taking all the feeling out of getting dressed. You'll gain a sense of control and ease as you learn to use your clothes to express yourself more confidently. The Style Formula gives you the guardrails to express your inner self in a way that works for you, so that you present and perceive yourself in a way you love. With this objectivity, you will then have the power to adapt your clothing to match your mood and needs.

That objectivity is also what makes the Style Formula so inclusive. It's based on geometry, symmetry, and balance. There are men with more stereotypically "feminine" traits, like a curvy waist, and there are women with more stereotypically "male" traits, like broader shoulders. The science looks only at the traits of the body—whether that body is male or female or nonidentifying does not matter. The point is to dress for your body science, combined with your personal preferences, allowing you to create the look you want. The Style Formula isn't restrictive—that applies to the people it works for as well. The science can be applied to anyone.

When you learn the components to create that harmonious look, you'll have mastered your Style ID—and then a whole new world of possibilities will be waiting in your closet.

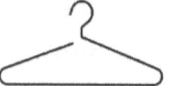

To the Closet: Take the First Step to Discovering Your Style ID

When working with my clients, we begin by determining their Style ID, which is derived from the components of the Style Formula. It's not like those reality shows you might remember, where a stylist comes swooping in and "edits" the wardrobe, throwing away half of it. I never start editing until we have the Style Formula down, because without the science that considers your body architecture, lifestyle, and preferences, it's impossible to properly edit for the unique preferences and needs of each client.

I like to go to the closet first, to give my clients an idea of how the science will inform their existing wardrobe. I usually start by requesting they go to their closet and pick something that they love and something that does not work for them.

I want them to start noticing the details of what they wear. What is it about that top that really works for them—the neckline, the length, the color? I'll ask them questions such as: "When it comes to the item that's not working, do you have an idea of why? Do you feel like it washes you out? Hits you in a way that makes you look shorter (or taller)? Does it hide a great feature?" As we start to answer those questions, we're getting into the science, without the client even realizing it. It is the first in a series of hands-on experiments.

I want you to do the same. You might be able to think of these items—the one you love and the one that just never seems to work. Maybe the one you love is that dress that always makes you feel great when you see yourself in the mirror. Maybe the one you struggle with is that blouse in a pattern you absolutely love but can never seem to create a complete outfit with, or never really feel good in when you put it on.

Right now, when you look at these two different pieces, they might not say much to you. However, they probably hold the secret to your Style ID. Take a photo of them with your phone. As we continue through the exercises in this book and start to understand the components of the Style Formula, you'll start to see the why of each of those pieces and view them through an objective lens. Let's put the Style Formula to the test. As we continue through the chapters of this book, we'll revisit these two pieces—and you'll probably see how they fit or don't fit your personal Style ID.

Unlock more style insights! Scan the QR code for exclusive content and interactive exercises to deepen your understanding of the chapter's key concepts and help you further explore your Style ID.

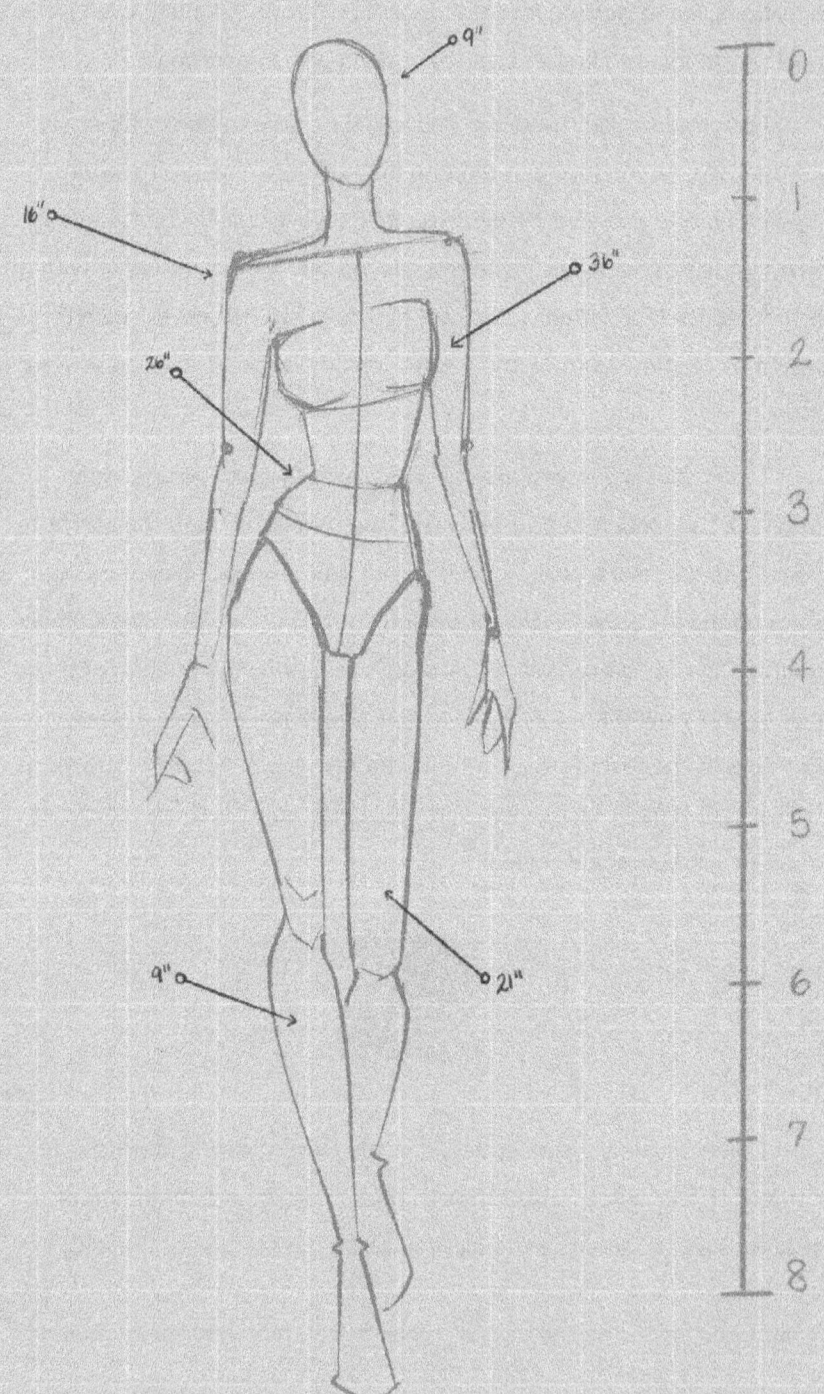

CHAPTER 2

Dressing for You

For many of us, whatever style we have is the product of our lives and preferences, shaped by years upon years of varied personal and societal influences—everything from friends to enemies, social media to magazines. Often, that style has evolved subconsciously, without us realizing its evolution. If we're going to unpack it, it's worth asking: How did we get here?

My personal preference had always been to dress "tough" to counteract my petite frame. I was always the smallest in the room—in school, in college, and later in business school, surrounded mostly by men. I tended toward severe cuts and dark colors. Anything that would make my petite frame look taller, more powerful, and less "cute."

Even when I was a kid, I shied away from being perceived as dainty. I grew up living the rural life, getting up at 5:00 a.m. to shovel horse stalls and tend to the animals. I didn't perceive myself as delicate, so I didn't want others to perceive me that way either. I had four brothers, and I wanted to be just like them. That meant I wanted to wear what they wore—ratty jeans and T-shirts and work boots. Back then, people would label me a tomboy. I just remember thinking, "They're all wearing this—I want to wear this too."

Around age eight, I learned how to sew my own clothes, something I continued through high school. Part of the reason I started sewing was because my mom tended to dress me in her very feminine style. I could wear my brother's overalls when I was mucking out the barn, but when we had a wedding or similar family event, I found myself in a fluffy dress or frilly skirt. I told myself it did not matter, but I never felt like myself in those styles. Sewing gave me more control over what I wore, allowing me to embrace the more sleek and simple pieces that I gravitated toward. In my mind, I was reacting to the expectations I felt to wear "girl" clothes. At the same time, by insisting on wearing "boy" clothes, I was admitting to myself and the world around me that the clothes *did* matter. I was too young to untangle the intricacies of that psychology then, but it makes me smile now.

When I tell you that I want you to dress for yourself, I mean it, because I've had my own experience of not being able to dress how I wanted. The issue came to a head in my tween years, when I grew more vocal about what I wanted to wear. My mom and I had our fair share of arguments about what was "appropriate" for Thanksgiving dinner or my uncle's wedding or my friend's birthday party. While I would have been content in ripped jeans and work boots, I knew that wasn't an option. Then, on one shopping trip—I think I was about twelve—my mom finally gave in and let me pick out some things I wanted. I remember exactly what I chose: a pair of paisley pants and a green sweater. I was thrilled. It was perfectly appropriate for the event, dressy enough to make everyone happy, but not frilly.

Back at home, I put on my new outfit and came downstairs. My mom, while not exactly thrilled with my choices, at least knew what to expect. But my dad had never imagined I wouldn't be in a pretty, frilly dress. He took one look at me and insisted I go change. I remember the argument that ensued vividly—my mom defending my choice, convinced that my outfit, though different from the usual, was perfectly appropriate, and my dad, standing firm, confused and adamant that I should be "properly dressed."

After more conversation—and a bit of shouting—my mom helped me explain that this wasn't about breaking rules but simply about exploring a new style that felt like me. The outfit suited the occasion; it just reflected a different side of me. Eventually, we all headed out, and for the first time, I felt truly comfortable and confident in what I wore. It was my first taste of just how empowering it is to wear clothes that reflect who you are.

Maybe you can remember this kind of experience from your own childhood. Or maybe you can remember something similar from your later years, when a well-intentioned friend or a magazine told you a certain article of clothing wasn't right for you—or perhaps, even more confusing, that something you did not like at all was perfect for you.

Like I said in the introduction, we all face a lot of external influences when it comes to what we wear. It's no wonder we are confused about our own style. The endless churn of contradictory advice and societal judgment can get in the way of the joy we find in our own personal style. However, it is possible to turn down the volume on all that noise, so that we can tune into what really matters—how we want to feel in what we wear. Let's start by unpacking some of the arbitrary rules that swirl around us all, every day.

Clothing as Visual Messaging, Then and Now

Clothes have long helped shape our societies. Take something as simple as a crown—it's an accessory, historically used to indicate royalty. Those kinds of social signifiers are outdated, but the significance of a crown is still immediately known to everyone.

Even if it's not as dramatic as a crown, everything we wear carries some visual message with it. Hairstyle, makeup, clothing, and accessories have all been shown to impact first impressions.[5] More generally, it's been suggested that a first impression is made within a tenth of a second of seeing someone's face—and that those first impressions are hard to shake once made.[6]

The formula I teach may be new—but people using clothing as visual messaging is not. Throughout history, clothing has been used to communicate everything from social class to gender roles, cultural identity, and resistance. Dress codes have been used to maintain social roles and hierarchies, with entire books written on the topic. For example, in nineteenth-century France, a person's identity was defined by social class affiliation, which was indicated by dress. While the fashion industry targeted the upper class, who relied on clothes to signal their status, the working class looked to clothing not for fashion but for function. A working-class man's suit, often purchased when he wed, was expected to last a lifetime, and worn not only for work but also for attending Sunday church, weddings, and funerals.[7]

Historically, people have also bent the rules of fashion as a form of resistance. During the Age of Enlightenment in Europe, for example, a simple business suit indicated a departure from earlier aristocratic

---

[5] Neil Hester and Eric Hehman, "Dress Is a Fundamental Component of Person Perception," *Personality and Social Psychology Review* 27, no. 4 (2023): 414-33, DOI: https://doi.org/10.1177/10888683231157961.

[6] Eric Wargo, "How Many Seconds to a First Impression?" Association for Psychological Science, July 2006, https://www.psychologicalscience.org/observer/how-many-seconds-to-a-first-impression.

[7] Melissa De Witte, "Dress Codes Can Reveal Social Aspirations, Political Ideals, Says Stanford Scholar," Stanford Report, February 2021, https://news.stanford.edu/stories/2021/02/dress-codes-reveal-politics-social-change.

regimes, which were characterized by opulent dress—a sign of status. On the other side of the ocean, much later, American civil rights activists of the 1960s purposefully wore their Sunday best to protests, a sign that they were worthy of respect and dignity, as they challenged the social and political hierarchies that kept them at the bottom.[8]

WEALTH AND SOCIAL CLASS

The link between clothes and money—and, by extension, social class—is nothing new. In the Elizabethan era, if you wanted to show how wealthy you were, your wig and makeup did the talking. Women would pin all their jewels onto their front to display their wealth. The Elizabethan era rules may be gone, but many still choose to use clothing to represent wealth and success, in creative or subtle ways.

Today, if you see someone wearing a Rolex, you immediately know it cost at least a few thousand dollars—more likely tens of thousands. Designer brands with obvious logos are another example. If you see someone in a plain white T-shirt, that doesn't mean much. If you see someone in a T-shirt with a Gucci logo on it, it's immediately clear to many that they spent a certain amount of money on it and want others to notice. On the other hand, there is quiet luxury, where people purposefully pay hundreds for a T-shirt with no logo whatsoever, because they don't want a brand reflected in their personal style.

People can use clothing to signify their wealth or status or to hide it. They may even use clothing as masquerade, presenting themselves as wealthy to the world with an expensive outfit—even if it is the only one in their closet. There's no right or wrong approach; the beauty of modern style lies in the freedom to choose how you express yourself.

---

8   Ibid.

GENDER ROLES

In the past, clothing has also helped to define gender roles in society. The Renaissance saw the emergence of padded doublets and codpieces worn by aristocratic men to exaggerate masculine features like broad shoulders and a genital bulge. This gender signaling showed status and power. In the Antebellum era, women wore hoopskirts to create an exaggeratedly small waist, a symbol of femininity. There have even been literal laws governing who could wear what, based on gender. In fact, women were once banned from wearing trousers in the US.[9]

In more recent decades, actual laws have been replaced by societal expectations and rules—some unspoken, others not. Now, even the societal rules around fashion are loosening up. Clothing is being used much more as a form of self-expression, which expands the choices in clothing pieces for everyone. There are no more rules around who can or cannot, or should or should not, wear certain clothing. We are all freer to express ourselves with a fluidity that's inspiring. Celebrities like Billy Porter and Harry Styles have walked red carpets in skirts, while cisgender women have graced magazine covers in tuxes. Younger generations are embracing the fluidity of clothing in a way that previous generations would or could not. There are still standards of formality for events, or professional dressing for work to reflect the company or the occasion, but how you do it is up to you.

GENERATIONAL IDENTITY

Clothes can also be a big indicator of generational identity. For example, the 1960s saw middle-class white youths adopting international fashions and hairstyles to signal a rejection of their parents'

---

[9] Madsen Pirie, "Who Was Wearing the Trousers," Adam Smith Institute, accessed October 16, 2024, https://www.adamsmith.org/blog/who-was-wearing-the-trousers.

values and to identify with counterculture politics. It was a shock to their parents, a more traditional generation. A young man letting his hair grow out in the 1960s was a far cry from the closely cropped haircuts men had in the 1940s and '50s. This is just one example of how younger generations may use clothes and style to push back against older generations.

It may be a universal truth that no generation wants to dress like their mom. These days, millennial women may cling to their skinny jeans, while Gen Z women may opt for wide-leg jeans. The funny thing is that generational styles become cyclical. You may very well one day find yourself dressing just like your mom did in her youth. Denim is a great example. Flared jeans were big in the 1970s. Then they cycled back in the 1990s. Now, they're back again in the 2020s. And those "mom jeans" came back into style around 2010. The term used to be an insult, but today younger generations are flocking to thrift stores for that high-waisted, pleated look.

The Mixed Messages of Modern Influences

A lot of the laws, rules, and dress codes of the past have gone away, leaving us with more choices—but also more confusion. We also have more visual messaging than in the past, from social media to video calls, not to mention the fact that everybody has a camera in their pocket these days. Some modern influences are adding to the noise, making getting dressed even more confusing than before:

FAST FASHION

The fashion cycle is moving faster now than ever before. With fast fashion and its incredible turnaround time, trends come and go with dizzying speed and have actually begun to overlap. Before ready-to-wear, it took months to get fabric and have a dress made. Even with ready-to-wear, it took manufacturers months or years to design, manufacture, and offer styles in stores. Now, it takes weeks. Fast fashion has also made clothing so cheap that we can and do buy more and more clothing, overfilling our closets with almost-right pieces that do not last. And because they do not last, we also end up contributing to overflowing landfills. Every year, Americans throw away more than 34 billion pounds of used textiles. Once discarded, 66 percent of clothing waste ends up in landfills.[10]

The fast-fashion industry does not want you to know how to dress yourself well, and with ease. Instead, it convinces us that we always need more. That if we just had the right jacket or the right pair of jeans or the right handbag, we would look and feel good. Everything would be okay. They want you to keep searching, to keep reaching, and, most importantly, to keep spending, always with the hope that the next thing you add to your closet is going to be the one that's going to make your world perfect. With your Style ID, you can step away from this cycle. No more overfilling closets with pieces you don't wear—just those that make you feel good. Your wardrobe becomes a curated selection that truly works for you, free from the endless chase.

"FASHIONABLE" BODIES

How we feel about our bodies tends to impact how we dress, and people often dress with their bodies in mind first. They want to make one thing look smaller or another thing look bigger—and often they are chasing not only fashion trends but also body trends, be it the waif of the 1990s supermodel or the curves of the Kardashians. Fashion-

---

[10] Dielle Lundberg and Julia DeVoy, "The Aftermath of Fast Fashion: How Discarded Clothes Impact Public Health and the Environment," BU School of Public Health, September 2022, https://www.bu.edu/sph/news/articles/2022/the-aftermath-of-fast-fashion-how-discarded-clothes-impact-public-health-and-the-environment/.

able body trends even have people paying for plastic surgeries. The Style Formula is not about changing your body. It's about objectively understanding the body you have and learning to artfully manipulate your look with your clothing choices. With your Style ID, you can craft your own visual messaging and present yourself as you want to be perceived.

There is a scene in the movie *Bride Wars* where Kate Hudson's character is trying on a Vera Wang wedding dress. The bridal shop assistant tells her, "You don't alter Vera to fit you; you alter yourself to fit Vera."[11] Meaning, if you don't fit the gown, you don't get it altered—instead, you lose weight. The message is that only people with specific proportions or a certain body type can wear Vera; everyone else who does not meet that idealized image is excluded.

This idea is still more broadly communicated to a lot of us: *we* need to change. In reality, it is the clothes that need to change. The Style Formula is your ticket out of the damaging cycles of fashion and "fashionable" bodies. Because once you have that formula in your back pocket, you will know how to build a wardrobe that works for your body and you will have the knowledge to put together outfits that you love and that reflect who you are.

MEDIA

Whether we consciously acknowledge it, the media constantly shows us visual images, suggesting we should look one way or another. In the past, it was print magazines, TV, and movies. Then, we added online blogs. These days, social media floods us with images that we are sometimes tempted to compare ourselves to. There have been countless studies on how media can alter self-perception. In the 1990s, those studies focused on fashion magazines. One exploratory analysis

---

11   *Bride Wars*, directed by Gary Winick (20th Century Fox, 2009).

of the time concluded that women who viewed fashion magazines were less satisfied with their bodies and more frustrated about their weight than their peers who viewed news magazines.[12] These days, such studies focus on social media, but the results are similar, suggesting that women who view images on social media are more likely to struggle with self-image.[13]

Again and again, research has shown that the images we see in the media can be tough on our self-esteem, with young people being especially affected. The good news is that some businesses are recognizing the implications and making changes, with major brands, from Victoria's Secret to Dove, trending toward body inclusivity in their representation in ads, fashion shows, and other marketing endeavors. Still, it's not the norm. With all that noise around us influencing our self-perception, we can easily end up missing out on appreciating the true beauty of our true bodies. Our bodies are amazing, and they allow us to do extraordinary things, from scaling mountains to creating and sustaining life. They literally keep us alive. And yet we can be so quick to critique them, when we should be critiquing the clothes or at the very least acknowledging that those "great jeans" just are not "great jeans for me." When we recognize it's in the jeans, not the genes, it gets easier to show ourselves some grace—and celebrate the clothes that do our bodies justice, while avoiding those that don't. This can be incredibly empowering and even help us break free of some of those outdated patriarchal, sexist, classist, or otherwise restrictive norms around dress—something Kathryn Nielsen, PhD, can attest to.

---

12   S. L. Turner, H. Hamilton, M. Jacobs, L. M. Angood, and D. H. Dwyer, "The Influence of Fashion Magazines on the Body Image Satisfaction of College Women: An Exploratory Analysis," *Adolescence* 32, no. 127 (1997): 604-14.

13   Just Say Yes, "Self-Esteem and Media Influences," May 2019, https://justsayyes.org/self-image-media-influences/.

CHAPTER 2

A Testament to the Power of Styling: Kathryn Nielsen, PhD, Senior Executive Officer, North Shore Community College

Kathryn and I have had many conversations about the evolving "rules" around expectations of dress. With her role in higher education, she's witnessing firsthand how younger generations are challenging societal norms. In this environment, it's critical to develop an approach that supports them as they navigate how to balance external pressures with their own desire to feel comfortable and confident in what they wear.

I've spent over twenty-five years working in higher education, an environment where the cycle of student development typically begins with the application process and culminates with career guidance as students prepare to enter the workforce. Within this cycle, career planning involves everything from networking and writing résumés and cover letters to participating in mock interviews. One key aspect of this preparation is advising students on what to wear—whether for interviews, internships, or co-op programs. Traditionally, this guidance has focused on the do's and don'ts of dress code, yet it's here that the politics of appearance truly come to the forefront. Higher education has long served as a battleground for culture wars, and as younger generations assert their rights to express their identities, we are being forced to rethink how we guide students and job seekers in choosing professional attire.

Fashion has always been an essential vehicle for social activism. Consider the time when women wearing pants was a revolu-

45

tionary act, challenging conventional gender norms. Today, as we've come to normalize pants for women, the next frontier of fashion activism may well lie in something as simple as pockets in women's clothing. Whether one is conforming to societal norms or rebelling against them, clothing is never neutral; it is always a statement. On one hand, you have students who are now prioritizing the question, "How do I want to express myself?" in their dress choices. On the other hand, the politics of appearance remain firmly in place—the fact is, how people dress often dictates how they are perceived and treated in professional spaces.

What I find so powerful about Aricia's approach is her ability to strip away the restrictive, internalized norms of patriarchy, sexism, and classism that typically govern how we think about dress. By focusing on the objective science of attire—such as proportions, color palettes, and fit—she moves beyond the outdated binary of "male" versus "female" attire. This allows individuals to express themselves in a way that feels most authentic and comfortable, without the constraints of traditional gendered expectations.

Aricia's method offers an inclusive, science-based approach to style that transcends traditional gender boundaries. I believe her techniques have great potential in higher education and the broader human resources field. Within my own sector, there is an increasing awareness of the need to rethink how we respond to and advise young people about professional dress—especially as they navigate the complex terrain of self-expression and identity.

For some individuals, particularly those who are trans or gender non-conforming, the question of "what to wear" becomes even more fraught. While Aricia's approach cannot solve all the societal challenges these individuals face, it provides a valuable tool for fostering more inclusive conversations. It helps people express themselves confidently and professionally, allowing them to embrace their identities through their clothing choices while remaining true to themselves.

Dressing for You, Now

The time for you to dress for yourself is now. The rules we used to be bound by are out the window. Take something like age-appropriate dressing. In the past, the expectations around what people wore at different life stages were more rigid. These days, there's much greater flexibility. When people ask me about what's "age appropriate," my answer is simple: any item is appropriate for your age, whatever age that may be. You can wear a mini skirt when you're twenty or when you're fifty or eighty. You might style it differently over the years, but there's no expiration date on the clothes you love.

Of course, every day we are all looking to balance expectations with reality. We all have roles or occasions for which we need to consider how to dress. We probably won't wear the same outfit to the beach as we wear to the office. Though at first glance that can feel like a constraint, once you know your Style ID, you can apply it in a way that allows you to feel comfortable with how you look and to express your individual style, wherever you are.

When I had my own children, it was important to me to let them exercise their self-expression, including in how they dressed. One of my children, Wesley, was born male and now uses she/her pronouns. I was thrilled when Wesley came to me in her twenties asking for help developing her personal style. We found ways for her to dress that were softer and more feminine, in line with her unique preferences.

I hope I can help you do the same. With so many outside influences giving us advice, opinions, and critiques, as well as our own inner voice adding to the opinions, it is no wonder it can be difficult for us to get dressed. It might seem overwhelming at first, but remember: knowledge is power. My journey to find what worked with my body and what reflected the real me is what became the Style Formula. With that in hand, you will know how to use clothing in a way that works for you—and allows you to express your authentic self.

I hope this book helps you discover a way to dress for your unique preferences, in a way that empowers you and brings you joy. In the chapters that follow, we'll cover the essentials of the Style Formula, including silhouette, color palette, and style personality as well as wardrobe building and outfit creation. Once you learn the Style Formula, you can dress yourself confidently and, I hope, with greater freedom than before—and have something to wear for every occasion.

I hope to empower you to tune out these external influences with the understanding of your Style ID. From magazine articles about what's age-appropriate to fashion blogs declaring what is and is not in at the moment, none of those things have a place in the Style ID. Forget the social media, the celebrities, the influences of your friends, family, partners, colleagues, people on the street.... Forget the past and the historical influences. This, right now, is your moment to express your true self.

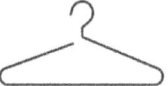

To the Closet: Get in Touch with Your Style Intuition

Dressing for yourself starts with *you*. Whatever you're wearing, you can make it yours. That goes beyond just your Style ID. It requires knowing what you love. It requires getting back in touch with that kid who played dress-up and looked in the mirror and never doubted that the toolbelt and pearls combo was so you. Authentically, truly you.

One way to get back into that mindset is to notice what you gravitate toward when you shop. What article of clothing or accessory attracts you like a moth to a flame? Ignore any rules or expectations or what you've been told before. Go with your gut instinct. When you walk through the flea market, take notice of that playful, bold scarf you like. If you're scrolling social media, save that post with those amazing wide-leg, hot-pink trousers. Those little moments when your gut instinct kicks in and you think, "That's so cool"—those moments are a nod to your personal sense of style.

It's like a style intuition, and that intuition sparks from the core of who you are as a person. Listening to that intuition is a way of expressing yourself more authentically. As we dive into the elements that create your Style ID, I want you to keep listening to that little voice inside of you—that gut instinct that kicks in when you really love something. Fine-tune that style intuition; let's start by finding something that sparks your style intuition right now.

At the end of the first chapter, I challenged you to go to your closet and pick out an item you loved and an item you didn't like. Head back to the closet, and this time pick out one piece of clothing that makes you feel powerful. Think: the chili pepper of your wardrobe. You wear it when you want to take charge. And then pick out one piece of clothing that makes you feel cozy. Think: the chicken soup of your wardrobe. You want to wear it to curl up at home with a good book or your favorite binge-worthy show.

Each of those articles of clothing makes you feel a certain way. Maybe your powerful item is a tailored blazer that makes you feel like a CEO. Maybe your cozy item is a sweater in a soft material. Take a photo of those articles. Remember how each makes you feel. As you explore the Style Formula, you'll want to refer back to items to remember: What resonated with you?

Unlock more style insights! Scan the QR code for exclusive content and interactive exercises to deepen your understanding of the chapter's key concepts and help you further explore your Style ID.

PART II
Discovering Your Style Elements

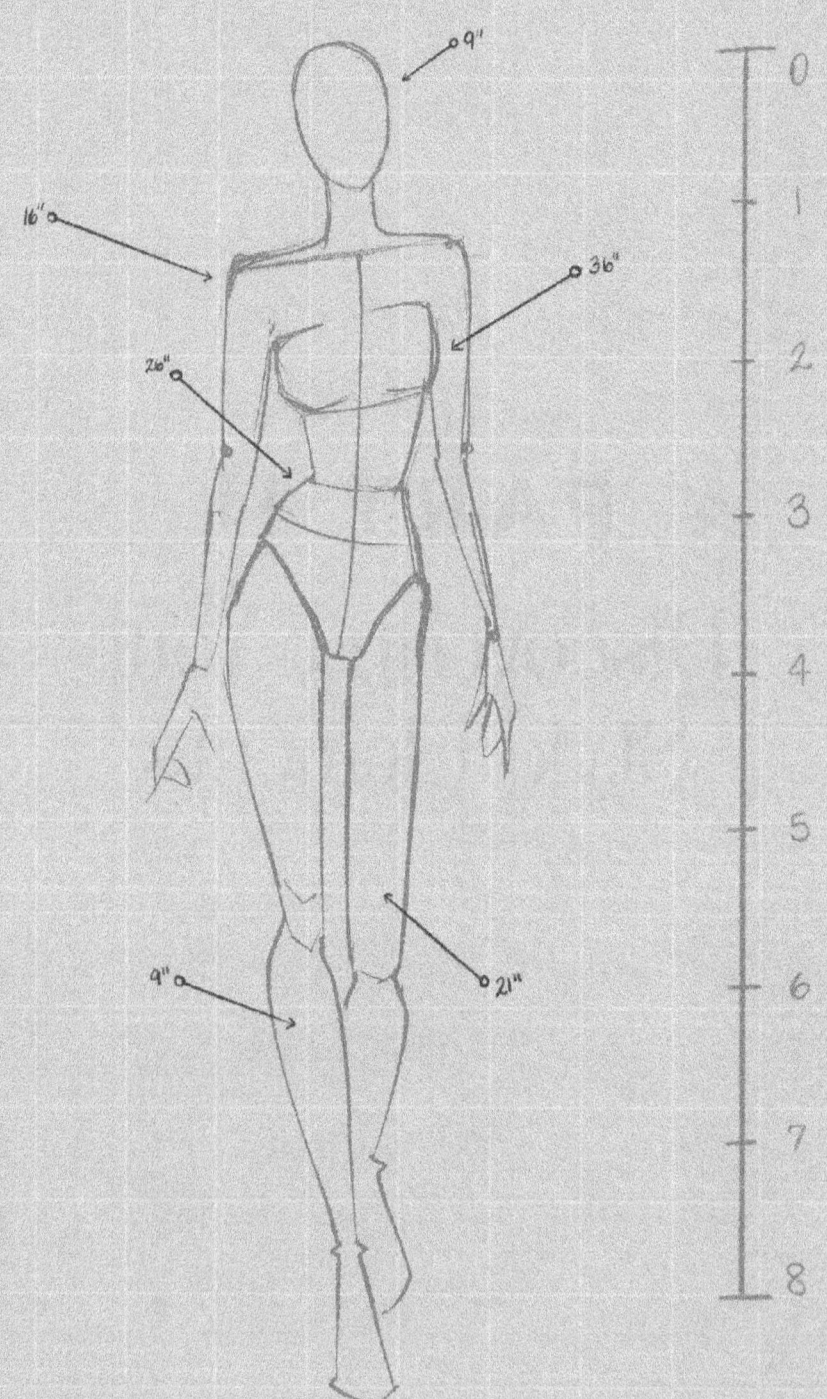

CHAPTER 3

Understanding Your Body's Architecture

I admit that it is inherently difficult to view one's own body objectively. I know even for myself there are days I am unwilling to face a mirror or feel I have "nothing to wear." That's why we turn to the Style Formula—beginning with body architecture, which provides objective measures of proportionality.

When I start talking about body architecture, a lot of clients think I'm talking about weight or size. Body architecture has nothing to do with either. It's about proportions, and how different parts of the body relate to one another. Once you have a sense of that for yourself, it's easier to turn down the volume on all that noise, external and internal, we just talked about. You can then use clothing to adjust your horizontal and vertical proportions in a way that fits your unique goals.

I'll never forget my client, Sarah, who came to me feeling utterly defeated.

"I just don't get my body," she admitted, sinking into a chair in my studio. "No matter what I wear, something feels off. I see all these women with my 'body type' looking amazing in certain outfits, but when I try them on, they just don't work."

She had read about body shapes online—hourglass, pear, rectangle—but none of those definitions helped her understand why clothes never looked the way she had envisioned.

Like many people, Sarah had never truly determined her own true proportions. As I began to explain the concept of body architecture, Sarah started to perk up. "So, you're saying it's like … a science?"

"Exactly!" I replied.*

As I grabbed my measuring tape and took her key bone structure measurements—shoulders, waist, hips—I saw a flicker of surprise in her eyes.

"Wait… my shoulders are actually wider than my hips? I always thought it was the other way around!"

I could see the frustration melting away, replaced by curiosity—and even relief.

I shared that many clients are surprised when they see their actual proportions measured objectively. That simple shift in understanding opened the door for Sarah to explore new styling possibilities—ones that truly worked for her.

It all starts with the simple science of measurements. By understanding your key measurements, you will gain an understanding of how your body is proportioned and form an image of that in your mind—much like sketching out your own Vitruvian man. The famous drawing by Italian Renaissance artist and scientist Leonardo da Vinci represents da Vinci's conception of ideal proportions.

CHAPTER 3

The Vitruvian person reveals the impact of proportions.

I have never had a client with these kinds of measurements. In reality, there are no ideal measurements. Creating balance in your visual architecture isn't about replicating da Vinci's ideal or any other. It's about understanding your horizontal and vertical proportions and how they work together. You have to consider both pieces of the puzzle, not just one or the other.

For example, a person with twenty-seven-inch shoulders and hips who is five feet tall will look different from a person with twenty-seven-inch shoulders and hips who is six feet tall. Both individuals have what is traditionally referred to as an "hourglass" figure, where the horizontal proportions are equal, with the shoulders and hips the same width. However, due to the height difference, they will look different, because their vertical proportions are different.

An hourglass figure can look very different on two different frames.

Even if the taller person had thirty-inch shoulders and hips, they would still be an hourglass shape, because the shoulders and hips are balanced—or, more specifically, the proportions of the two are balanced.

I often compare body architecture to the frame of a house. Body architecture is essentially your bone structure, and, just like the frame of the house, this underlying structure does not change, for the most part, throughout your life. This is something my clients are often surprised to learn: your body architecture stays the same. It doesn't matter if you gain weight or lose weight, get pregnant, build muscle, or even get plastic surgery. It's like the frame of a house—it remains the same even when you renovate other parts, like the floors or roof. The frame, its bones, are not altered in the process. Yes, the body may change. Weight gain can result in a wider waist, for example. But that won't alter the balance of the hips and shoulders, which are the frame that determines proportionality.

Once you understand your body architecture, you can move beyond the basic structure and think about details. If we're comparing it to building architecture, it's like considering how windows and doors influence the feeling of a room. For instance, a room with high ceilings can feel intimate and cozy with lower doors and windows, or it can be made to feel grand and awe inspiring with extra-tall ones. Architects know how to play with space and make choices to shape both a room's look and atmosphere. In the same way, once you understand the frame of your house, your bone structure, you gain the insight to make nuanced choices that influence how you present yourself.

Understanding Horizontal and Vertical Proportions

There are all sorts of systems and methods that have been developed to label bodies according to how they are balanced. You have probably seen magazines, blogs, or social media posts refer to women as pieces of fruit (apple, pear, etc.) or shapes (rectangle, triangle, wedge, etc.). At this point, many of those labels come with assumptions and implied meanings that can too easily open the door to comparison. Focusing on body architecture moves us away from the subjectivity of those labels and toward objectivity, creating clarity. And once you understand body architecture, you can learn how to manipulate it.

There are many tools to help you manipulate the appearance of your architecture. For example, if you want to add interest to the bottom portion of your frame, you might wear pants in a vibrant color. Alternatively, you could create more visual weight—a design principle that draws the viewer's attention—by using texture. A tweed skirt with a nubby texture, for instance, adds more visual weight than a smooth cotton skirt. Cut can also be used to add or subtract visual weight. For instance, wide-leg pants will add more visual weight to the bottom half of the body than straight-cut pants, which are more streamlined. These are just a few examples, and we will talk more about how to create balance through things like shapes, color, and texture in the next chapter.

First, we want to determine the architecture you have, your frame of reference. Then, we'll explore various tools to modify balance and create the look you want. In general, balancing the silhouette creates a form of symmetry that visually elongates the frame, creating a more streamlined appearance. You can also choose to intentionally create an unbalanced silhouette. Some people may want to add curves or volume to their upper body, while others might prefer to emphasize their lower half. The beauty of understanding your shape is that you can highlight specific areas as you wish, shaping your look to reflect your unique preferences.

When you complete the exercise at the end of this chapter, you will have a better understanding of your body architecture and can create, mentally, your own Vitruvian person. You will understand not only your horizontal but also your vertical proportions, and how the different parts of your body relate to one another. Which parts of you are broader or narrower? Shorter or taller? How do those portions of your body relate to one another? Knowing the answers to these questions will help guide you as we move ahead in the book and learn how to play with proportions and balance using clothing and all its varied characteristics—cut, color, texture, pattern, and more.

When working with clients, one of the first steps is taking measurements at bone structure points. This is the basis to understanding their body architecture. It is always interesting to see clients' reactions as they see these objective measurements. Many have assumed certain things about their architecture and are surprised by the actual numbers. Even with the evidence right in front of them, many clients find it hard to reconcile with their own perceptions. Their inner voice and ingrained beliefs about their shape can be so powerful that they remain convinced, for example, that their hips must be the widest point of their body—even as I'm there with a measuring tape, showing them otherwise.

For us to be able to create or maintain the balance we want, we need to first understand the balance we have. That is why measurements are so important. The conclusion of this chapter includes an activity so that you can take your own measurements to better understand your horizontal and vertical proportions. For now, I want to talk a bit more about what I mean with these terms and why they matter.

HORIZONTAL PROPORTIONS

Horizontal proportions focus on the balance or width relationship between the dominant horizontal points of the body: the shoulders, waist, and hips. Determining how the three relate to one another is the key—is one point wider or narrower than another, or are they the same? We start by determining the width of the shoulders and the hips and then determine the waist's width relative to the shoulders and hips—is the waist wider, similar to, or narrower? The numbers themselves don't matter. What matters is the balance or width relationship of the three.

Horizontal proportions can be balanced in any combination of the three, for example:

- The shoulders are broader than the hips.
- The hips are broader than the shoulders.
- The shoulders and hips are equally broad.
- The midsection is the broadest point.

However your proportions align, what matters is simply understanding the balance of your body—your architecture.

CHAPTER 3

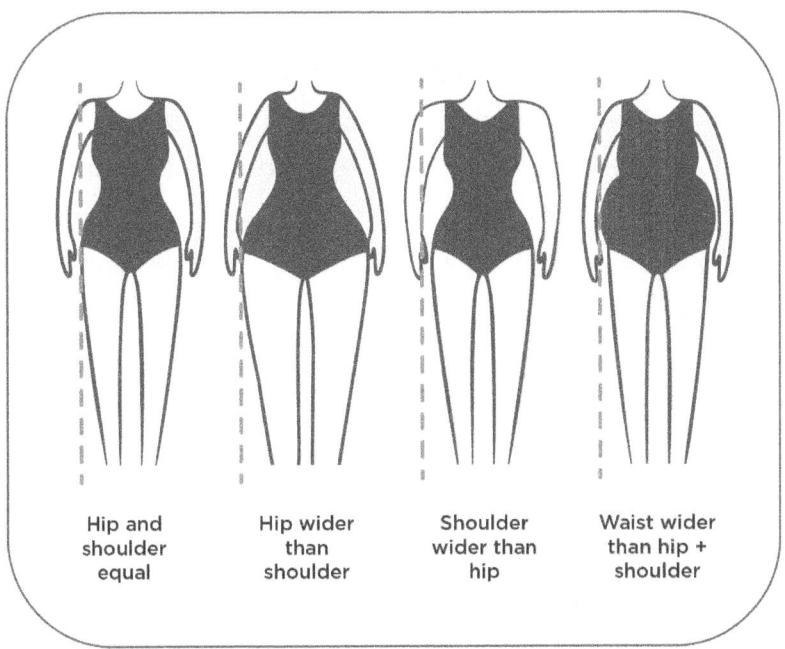

Types of horizontal proportions

Think of it in terms of silhouette. If you are standing in front of even light, and your shadow is cast directly on the wall behind you, which of the three dominant horizontals of the body is the widest? This is a simple way of figuring out how your horizontal proportions relate to one another.

The age-old example of stripes is a good case study for how the clothing you wear can influence the appearance of your visual architecture. If you want to elongate your body visually, you wear vertical stripes, keeping the eye moving up and down the body. Horizontal stripes, on the other hand, visually cut across the body, stopping the eye from moving up and down, creating a shortening (and widening) effect.

VERTICAL PROPORTIONS

Body architecture also considers your vertical proportions, where you are longer and where you are shorter up and down the body. Vertical proportions might also be called linear proportions. This is something that many body-typing methods don't address. Vertical proportions are just as important as horizontal proportions in creating balance. Focusing on just one or the other doesn't give you the full frame of the house.

Also, importantly, vertical proportions as seen in the Vitruvian model are often used in the manufacturing of clothing, not because anyone actually has these exact proportions but because it is used as an estimate or averaging of bodies, which is what ready-to-wear (clothing that is mass produced and sold in stores, rather than made to order) is all about. Understanding vertical measurements is thus especially useful for shopping—helping us to understand the proportions we have in relation to the proportions of clothing.

The key vertical proportions to note are:

- Short or long waist: the distance from the midbust to the waist.
- Short or long rise: the distance from the waist to the crotch.
- Short or long legs: the distance from the crotch to the floor (midpoint of the body).

Every person's architecture is uniquely their own. The goal is simply to understand your proportions, so you can manipulate them as you wish.

CHAPTER 3

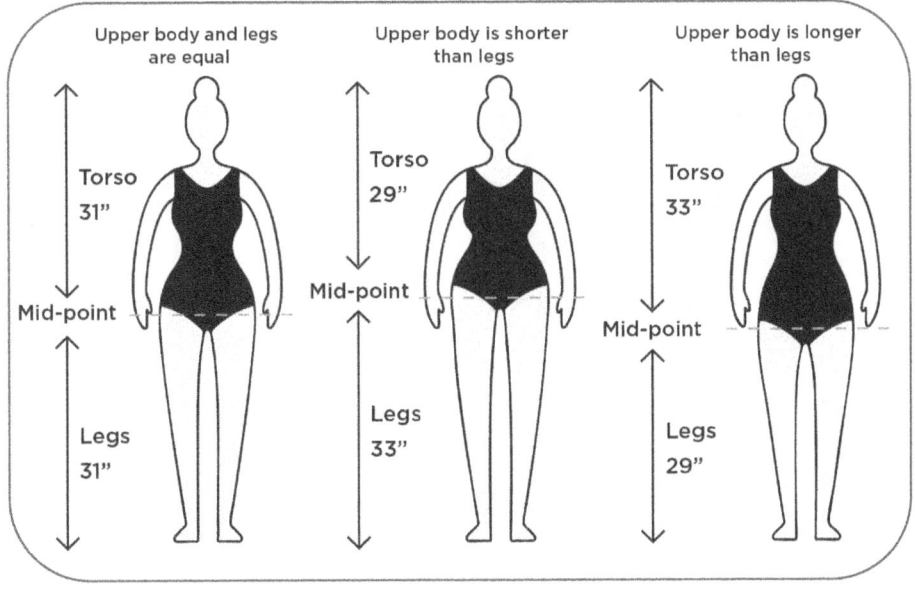

Some of the most useful vertical proportions on figures of equal height

Top lengths are an easy way to show how impactful vertical proportion can be. Where a top hits on the body creates a visual cut across your vertical proportions. If your top ends at the low hip, this cut makes your legs appear shorter and your upper body appear longer. If your top is shorter and ends higher up on the hip, it elongates the legs. Horizontal lines like hemlines, belts, crops, and similar all impact the balance of your visual vertical architecture.

Understanding Vertical Proportions

An example of how to manipulate vertical proportions with lines. In which image do the legs look longer?

Skirts and dresses, and where they land, are also a good example. If you have shorter legs, and you hem your skirts a little bit shorter, there is more skin showing, which gives the illusion of an elongated leg. Waistbands make a difference too. A person with shorter legs might opt for a higher waistband to make the bottom half of their body look longer. However, a person with long legs may not like the look of high-waisted pants, because they make the already long legs look even longer, while shortening the top half of the body—throwing things off balance.

CHAPTER 3

Learning How to Modify Your Body Architecture

Once you have identified your body architecture, you will have the power to balance or unbalance it exactly how you like. I have short legs and a long torso, for instance. When I want to make my legs look longer, I wear high-waisted pants. People will often say to me, "Your legs are so long" when I wear these pants. That isn't the case at all. I just have an understanding of my body architecture and how to dress for it. My legs may look long and give the impression of a tall frame; in reality, I am only 5'2".

Similarly, I avoid low-waisted pants, which tend to further elongate my torso and make my legs look even shorter. However, if I wanted to elongate my midsection or waist area, I would reach for a pair of midrise pants—this allows me to "borrow" some of the extra space of my longer torso to elongate my waist without shortening my legs.

I know how to manipulate my vertical proportions like this because I have a clear understanding of my body architecture. That's what allows me to design the look I want. I wasn't born with this knowledge. It was not something that ever crossed my mind when I was mucking around in the barn as a kid or trying to look tough in business school. I learned it later in life—and now I use it all the time. You can do the same. Once you learn your own body architecture (and remember you only have to learn it once), you will be able to play with proportions in a way that makes you happy.

It's about changing the clothes, not about changing yourself. In some cases, this may mean altering great clothes you already have to better fit your architecture. When my kids were younger, I used to hem their baseball shirts myself. Otherwise, they had their jerseys hanging halfway down their thighs or bunched up in their pants, with what seemed like forty feet of fabric stuffed into their waistband. I am not saying you have to fire up the sewing machine yourself; there are tailors who can do the job and, especially for staple pieces, like the perfect pair of pants, it can be worth the investment—something we'll explore further in chapter 7, all about building a wardrobe.

In the next chapter, we'll get into greater detail about how to manipulate your horizontal and vertical proportions, creating balance in your looks through shape, color, and texture. Here, I want to focus on manipulating your proportions using lines—both horizontal and vertical. Basically, it comes down to where you are creating lines on your body and how those lines impact your silhouette.

For example, I like to create more balance with my wider shoulders by accentuating my hips. I do this by wearing a color-contrasting layer, creating a horizontal line at the hips that makes them appear visually wider. It's not about making the hips look bigger but about creating overall balance with the shoulders. Simply layering a pink T-shirt with blue jeans has a similar effect; where that T-shirt hem ends is going to create a horizontal line. That is why monochromatic dressing tends to elongate your frame and make you look taller, because you are getting rid of all the horizontal lines in an outfit.

Once you start to look for these lines, they will probably jump out at you all the time. You will see how a cropped pant cuts the leg line. Ankle straps on a shoe also create a visual break, at the ankle line. If you pair a cropped pant and ankle-strap shoes, you are cutting your leg visually in two places, shortening its appearance. Similarly, if you're wearing all black and put on a red jacket, you are creating a line that essentially cuts your body in half.

It's easy to experiment with this any time you're in your closet. Put on a big T-shirt or sweatshirt, along with a color-contrasting bottom, and pull the top tight so the bottom hits at different points of your body—low on the hips versus the waist. Notice how the eye follows the visual "cut" made in the color contrast of the top and bottom. Move the line around to see where you like it. This is one step to appreciating how you are in control of the clothes. In the next chapter, we'll talk more about ways to exercise that control.

Body Architecture: The Frame of Your House

In styling, the concept of "symmetry" is often better described as balance, and clothing is an incredible tool for creating and modifying this balance in any way you choose. You invest in your clothes, so make them work for you. Traditionally, styling focused on creating as much balance as possible, with elongating and slimming being the ideal goal. But today, I believe there is no single ideal standard of beauty—each body is beautifully unique, and each of us gets to decide how we want to dress.

Maybe you prefer not to seek balance. Maybe you want to accentuate your bust or your bottom. Whatever your preference, with the knowledge in this book and the tools of clothing and accessories, you'll be empowered to shape your look how you like. My goal is to guide you in mastering this for yourself. The first step is figuring out your body architecture. All you need is a tape measure.

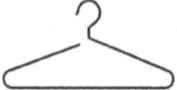

To the Closet: Take Your Measurements

Ready to create your own Vitruvian person? Before we start measuring, I want you to take a guess: Which of the three horizontal proportions do you think is the widest measurement? Your shoulder, waist, or hips? And now, do you think you have long legs or short legs? Let's record a few key measurements that will give an idea of your body architecture.

Grab a builder's tape measure or yardstick, since these measurements are best done with a stiff tape measure, not a soft sewing tape measure. Use a mirror that is not slanted or leaning at an angle but is flat against a wall and stand in front of the mirror, facing it straight on.

As you do this, wear fitted clothing without shoes and stand up straight with your arms to the side as much as possible.

Horizontal Proportions

Place the tape measure horizontally across each area, touching the body, but do not bend the tape measure. Fill in each measurement below:

1. **Shoulders:** Measure across the widest point of the shoulder area. Slide the tape measure up and down the body to find the widest spot while keeping the top of the arms at your sides as much as possible. Note your measurements: _____

2. **Waist:** Measure across the smallest point of your natural waist. The natural waist is the place that indents when you stand up straight and bend to the side. Slide the tape measure up and down to find the smallest point. _____

3. **Hip:** Measure across the widest part of the hip. Slide the tape measure up and down to find the widest point. _____

Which of these three measurements is the widest or narrowest—or are some equal? With your measurements in hand, go back to your guess at the top of the exercise. Were you right? Or did you have any misconceptions about your body architecture?

Vertical Proportions of the Legs

Place the tape measure vertically with the zero at the floor and measure up while not bending the tape measure. Fill in the two measurements below:

1. **Height:** You probably already have a rough idea of your height. To get it just right, you can measure it again now from the floor to the top of the head. You can place a ruler or flat object on your head to more easily find the top and use the mirror to help you see your measurement: _____

2. **Legs:** Measure from the floor up to your crotch to determine your leg length. _____

Next subtract your leg measurement from your height to determine if your legs are longer, shorter, or the same length. So, if you are sixty inches tall, and your legs are twenty-eight inches, then your torso is thirty-two inches—meaning your legs are shorter than your torso. If your legs are shorter than your torso, you have proportionately short legs. If they are longer, you have proportionately long legs.

With your measurements in hand, go back to your guess at the top of the exercise. Were you right? Or did you have any misconceptions about your body architecture? Now, you have the objective figures in front of you.

Unlock more style insights! Scan the QR code for exclusive content and interactive exercises to deepen your understanding of the chapter's key concepts and help you further explore your Style ID.

CHAPTER 4

Modifying Balance Through Cut, Color, Texture, and More

A lot of my clients are excited to jump right into closet editing when we work together. It's a natural inclination. But first, I want to get to know the client—not only characteristics like body architecture, but also their style goals. With this insight, we can make meaningful edits that align with what they want to achieve.

I had a client—I will call her Maria—who was especially eager to get to the closet edit. As soon as we'd taken her measurements and determined her body architecture, she was enthusiastically guiding me to her closet to take a look. Maria's measurements showed that her shoulders were broader than her hips, and she shared that she always felt like her shoulders dominated her frame, making her look bigger than she was. When we talked about her style goals, Maria expressed that she wanted to downplay her shoulders. What she was really communicating to me, without realizing it, was that she wanted a more balanced appearance; she wanted to add visual weight on the bottom, not the top.

Then, we stepped into her closet. She had a lot of amazing options and started pulling out a variety of tops—different brands, price points, colors, cuts, patterns, and materials. As she went through, she told me which ones she liked and which ones she didn't like and a few that she was unsure about. Soon, we had an array of tops laid out in front of us. I reminded her, "You mentioned wanting to soften the look of your shoulders. Let's go through each of these pieces together with that in mind and see what each will do toward that goal."

We started sifting through tops together. We pulled a boatneck top first. She loved the color but mentioned that she hardly ever wore it, so I asked her to put it on. I could see in her face that she wasn't happy with how it looked. I wanted to help her understand *why* it didn't feel right to her. We began by looking at the cut. I explained, "This neckline creates a horizontal line right across your shoulders, moving the eye from side to side, making the shoulders look wider, calling attention to them." I could see the glimmer of recognition start to flicker in her eyes. I then asked her—while she was wearing the boatneck shirt—to take the neckline and pull it down, to create a V-neck effect. The change was instant: the V-neck created a vertical line that not only broke up the horizontal line of the boatneck but also broke up the strong horizontal created by her shoulders, making them appear less broad. Her face lit up. That's when the glimmer of recognition in her eyes became a spark of excited knowledge. She got it.

She went back to the tops we'd laid out and started picking through them: "This one has horizontal stripes, so that's going to make my shoulders look broader. And this one is in a bright color and has a shiny satin fabric, so that's going to attract attention to my top half as well. And this one is blousy and drapey, which I thought would hide my shoulders, but it just makes my shoulders look big while concealing my curves."

It was one of those moments I love as a stylist: I saw it click for my client, and she was able to figure out exactly what would and would not serve her. Maria knew her style preference, and she had the right idea in realizing that the shirt she picked could help her achieve that preference. What she didn't have was an understanding of her own body architecture and, given that, how to use clothes to match her style preferences. We worked together so she could do just that.

This chapter explores how you can do the same for yourself. You will learn how something as simple as changing a neckline can dramatically impact the balance and overall look of an outfit. My goal is to empower you to take control over your style by understanding how clothing interacts with your unique shape, giving you the confidence and control to dress with ease. So that you, like Maria, can experience that glimmer of "I got it" excitement in your eyes.

Tools You Can Use to Manipulate Visual Balance

Each piece of clothing you wear has some impact. The whole idea behind styling is to understand what each piece is doing. The impact will vary according to its features like cut, color, and texture, as well as according to your own Style ID, from your proportions to your skin tone. You can use this knowledge to achieve the look you want.

When you see how something as simple as the texture of a fabric can change the visual balance of an entire look, you will start to understand how the choices you make when dressing shape the final outcome. Here, we look at modifying balance with cuts, colors, prints, textures, and details and embellishments.

CUT

Both the overall shape of a garment and the outline it creates can visually influence body architecture. Say you want to play up your shoulders. A structured blazer with shoulder pads widens the shoulder line, adding literal structure and width. Meanwhile, a boatneck creates a horizontal line that visually broadens the area, moving the eye side to side. Alternatively, if you wanted to soften or narrow a broad shoulder or lessen the visual weight of the shoulder, you might wear a V-neck top or a pendant necklace. This creates a V at the shoulders and breaks up the strong horizontal line of the shoulders. I have encountered clients with broad shoulders who refuse to wear halter tops, because they don't want to highlight their broader shoulders. In fact, the lines of a halter top can break up the shoulder visually, softening it and allowing the area to be shown off visually in a way that works for them.

Another example: if you want to add visual weight to the bottom half of your body, you might wear a skirt that flares out slightly. In this case, you are using shape to modify your horizontal proportions. And naturally, when you emphasize or deemphasize one part of your body, it has a corresponding effect on other areas. Adding visual weight to your hips, as just described, contributes to deemphasizing your shoulders.

Once you understand the power of shape, you can learn how to use it to modify or match your body architecture. My personal example is the baby-doll dress. A baby-doll dress is a short dress that's fitted at the bust and then bells out into a loose and flowy garment with lots of volume. I thought it was a whimsical trend and wanted to try it out, but I knew the traditional cut would not work for my body architecture. Instead of writing off the trend, I realized I could adapt it by wearing an empire waist instead. An empire-waist dress is likewise fitted at the bust but instead of billowing out into a short bell, it cascades down and skims the body. This was a take on the baby-doll dress trend that worked for my body and my preferences. I still achieved the basic shape created by a baby-doll look, but in a way that I liked for myself.

COLOR

Another way you can create and modify balance is with color. If you want to add visual weight to something and emphasize it, you can use colors that have a lot of visual weight. All colors have visual weight of some kind. For example, black pants have less visual weight than red pants. The eye will land on bright red before it lands on black. The question of "Where does my eye land first?" is a good way to determine visual weight.

Visual weight is also relative—it depends on what else you are wearing. When a fashion magazine tells you that black pants are slimming, that's not really giving you enough information to work with. Are you pairing the black pants with a top that has more or less visual weight than the pants? That is what will determine where the eye goes. And it does not have to be black pants. In fact, any pant that is darker than the top you choose will have the same effect of creating less visual volume on your lower compared to your upper half. So, if you pair a dark-denim bottom with a bright-red top, the eye naturally goes to the red top because it has more visual weight. Add a colorful scarf and that weight increases even more. But if you switch to a black top, the eye shifts downward to the more comparatively interesting dark-blue denim, making your lower half the focal point.

So there's no need to stick to black pants to downplay the lower body. Any darker color on the bottom paired with a lighter, more eye-catching top can achieve the same effect, including the lighter colors we reach for in summer. A stark white is going to be a lot brighter and more visually interesting than a muted khaki. That's why I often suggest clients pair camel or khaki pants with a white top in the summer instead of dark, heavy black pants. The white top is adding lots of visual weight to the upper half of the body, naturally drawing the eye away from the "still darker but not black" lower body. This is a great combination for someone who wants to emphasize their shoulders, or balance wider hips without relying on black for contrast.

I have had clients who want to downplay their lower half tell me that they avoid bright-colored pants entirely. I reassure them, "You can wear brick-red pants! If you want to balance your silhouette, simply pair those pants with an optic white top, which is bright and adds visual weight to the top." It's all about balance.

PRINTS AND PATTERNS

Prints and patterns are another tool you have at your disposal for adding or detracting visual weight. Generally speaking, a piece of clothing that features a print or pattern will have more visual weight than an item with no print. And darker and quieter prints with less contrast and color tend to have less visual interest, while brighter and busier prints with more contrast and colors have more. If you have a gray pant with an all-over blue paisley print, that is going to have more visual interest than a plain gray pair of pants. Similarly, a plain light-pink top has less visual interest than a light-pink top with white polka dots all over it. Even a navy-blue pant with slightly darker navy-blue stripes or swirls will have more visual interest than a pair of plain navy pants. The pattern keeps the eye moving over the fabric, darting around and attracting attention.

If you wanted to balance broader hips and smaller shoulders, you might wear a print top with plain blue jeans on the bottom. Many patterns have some color in them, so you may even end up combining the visual impact of color and print in one article of clothing.

The placement of prints also plays a role. Some prints repeat a design across a whole garment. Other prints are placed only on one part of a garment or have variations across different parts of the garment. This also influences where the eye travels over the body. A plain tee with flowers on the shoulders will emphasize and visually broaden the shoulders, while a tee with a bold print running across the bottom hem will emphasize the hips. As you learn how patterns add or take away visual weight, you can use them to create a variety of balanced looks.

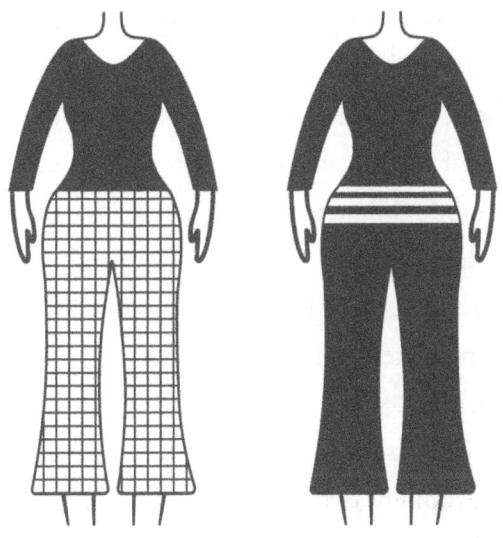

Pattern and detail draw the eye, creating more visual weight

With patterns especially, there are so many fun possibilities: paisley, polka dot, gingham, floral, windowpane, tartan—and the list goes on. That does not mean you have to pursue patterns in your outfits. I have had clients who simply do not like patterned clothes. They prefer the clean look of solids and rely on accessories or cut to add interest and play with balance. If you are drawn to prints, trust your instincts and seek out ones you love—look for those that speak to you. There are many ways to manipulate visual balance, so you can choose the tools that best suit your preferences and bring you the most enjoyment. This is just one of the many tools available for creating the look you want.

TEXTURE

Texture is another characteristic of clothing that can add or take away visual weight. A nubby sweater is going to have more visual weight than a plain, smooth, long-sleeve cotton jersey shirt, because the material is bulkier and adds volume. So, if I want to downplay my top half, I'll stick to minimal, nontextured fabrics for tops, and then I might add visual weight on the bottom with a textured fabric like tweed. If I want to highlight my shoulders, for instance, I might wear a bouclé or corduroy jacket.

This is also a consideration in other areas, like footwear. Take boots, for example. Suede tends to be soft and matte and disappears, whereas the sheen on leather gives it a lot of visual interest, especially if the leather is very shiny. One of my clients learned this subtle difference when she bought two pairs of black leather boots, one pair in suede and another in a shiny leather. The boots were the exact same size, style, brand, everything—the only difference was the material. She told me, "I love the suede ones. But I feel like the other pair makes my feet look huge." The difference was the material; the shiny leather was drawing attention to her feet, which she didn't want, while the matte suede had a subtler effect.

She had missed the return window on the boots, so we explored ways she could wear them. We went through her closet and found a pair of awesome red pants she already owned, which added visual weight to her legs, balancing out the visual weight the boot was giving the foot. Cumulatively, by pairing other items, we were able to create the balanced look she was after.

DETAILS AND EMBELLISHMENTS

Last but not least, details and embellishments are a great way to play with balance. Say you want to add more visual weight to your bottom half, but you generally like to just wear jeans. You don't have to go out and buy a pair of hot-pink pants to achieve the effect you're after. Instead, you might look for jeans with whiskering across the hips and thighs (whiskering is the faded horizontal creases that form on jeans). Alternatively, you might look for decorative stitching or embroidery on the pockets.

You can also look beyond pants to add visual weight to the bottom. You might get a blazer with large pockets set exactly at the hip, for instance, directing the eye downward and adding visual interest to the hips and lower body. Conversely, if you want to detract attention from the hips or create less visual interest, you might instead wear a blazer with slit pockets or no pockets at all.

These kinds of details impact the overall balance of any outfit, and once you start paying attention to them and the effect they have, you will be able to put together outfits that serve you well in a controlled, deliberate way. It can be very freeing once you realize the huge variety of details and how you can manipulate them to create the balance you are after: zippers, buttons, eyelet hooks, stitching, embroidery, pockets, patches, sequins, jewelry, and accessories—these can all attract attention and change your visual balance.

As you come to understand the difference that each element can make in terms of visual balance, you will have a lot more freedom to play around with that balance. By learning the why, you can figure out the what. I'm not here to give you the rules but to give you the tools. And I want that tool kit to be as comprehensive as possible.

As you start to see all the possibilities you have in your closet, you're probably starting to feel a bit freer. Maybe some of the frustration you have been feeling about getting dressed is starting to fade, as the pieces of the puzzle fall into place.

Modifying Balance Requires a Holistic Approach

Now that you have begun to consider the idea of visual weight, it will be easy to recognize. The end-of-chapter exercise will also help you fine-tune that skill. Of course, there's an interplay throughout all of this. If I wear a smooth, nontextured top, but it has a brick-red plaid print, that top is still going to have a lot of visual weight. You want to think about all the different elements that add and detract visual weight and how they work together. It's similar to interior design. When you walk into a room with a Christmas tree, sparkling and full of lights, that's likely the first thing that will catch your eye. Your gaze isn't going to gravitate toward the gray trash cans, which are designed to blend in against the background of the gray wall and carpet.

Take a silk blouse, for example. Silk is a smooth, nontextured fabric, which makes it seem like it would not add a lot of visual weight—but it can also have some shine to it, which adds visual weight. Similarly, if you have a silk blouse in a muted creamy white, it's going to have less visual weight than a silk blouse in a stark optic white. If that silk blouse has a widespread collar, that draws attention to the shoulder and adds visual interest. If it has giant shoulder pads, that can significantly change the shape of the blouse and add visual weight on the top.

Elements like lines, color, and texture can also be used to highlight or camouflage specific areas of the body. For example, if you want to camouflage or downplay the bust, you could break up the bust area with a V-neck-cut top or wear darker colors on top. This approach will also downplay the shoulders. If you don't want to downplay the shoulders, you might opt for a V-neck with cap sleeves. On the other hand, you may prefer to highlight or enhance your bust by adding texture, such as ruching or pockets set at the bust. Or simply wearing a pendant necklace that lands directly on your bust also adds visual interest and enhances the area.

Again, the question of, "Where does the eye land?" can guide you here. You can draw the eye to one area and away from another area by adding something eye-catching with visual interest. That visual interest could come from the color or pattern, for example, or even the texture. You can also use scale. Surround an area you want to downplay with something larger, so that the area you want to attract less attention to appears smaller. You can wear a wide-flared sleeve to make an upper arm appear smaller, for instance—it's all about what you want.

This might seem like a lot to think about. As with any new skill, practice makes perfect. I promise you: it will become second nature as you start to "see like a stylist" with your newfound knowledge. And that knowledge is going to put you in control. And remember, you only need to focus on the information that is relevant to *you*.

If you took your measurements in the previous end-of-chapter exercise and discovered that your shoulders are broader than your hips, and you want to bring more balance to your appearance, then you only need to focus on the tools that will let you do that. You know you want to add visual weight on the bottom or minimize visual weight on the top, so you might look for bright A-line skirts, wide-legged print pants, and denim with decorative pockets. You know you want to avoid adding visual weight to the top, so you might avoid puff sleeves or bright colors and patterns in your shirts. Or, if you love colorful tops, then you might balance a bright top with lots of interest on the bottom.

As you start to put together individual pieces and create outfits, the importance of taking a holistic approach will become even clearer. We're going to talk more about putting together outfits in the final chapter—that is, after all, the goal of this book. My hope is that you will take what you've learned about the elements of the Style Formula and be able to sift through your wardrobe and easily recognize what pieces truly work for you.

As you learn more about your proportions and the tools available to you to manipulate proportions, you can also start to think about your style preferences. In Maria's case, she knew she wanted to downplay her shoulders, but she wasn't sure how to get there. She came to realize that what she was really after was a more balanced appearance. She had so many of the pieces she needed already in her closet. It was just a matter of learning what impact different pieces would have on her unique proportions and then pairing them in ways that aligned with her preferences.

Also, those preferences can change. The goal is to empower you to take control of dressing yourself for any occasion or any mood. Maybe you want to wear a more balanced look in a professional setting, for example, but on the weekends, you want to draw attention to your curvy bottom. With knowledge of your Style ID, you will be able to do both.

As you start playing with proportions, you can also consider the creative side. There are so many ways to alter balance, from textures to colors and cuts. Considering what you like in these terms will help you create balance in a way that you love. This creative part is just as important a part of the style journey.

Best of all, you'll be able to do it with ease—and speed. No more standing in front of the open closet, with clothes strewn about, trying to determine what pants to wear with what top, or which skirt to wear with which blouse. As you start to put the above principles into practice, you will have a closet full of clothes that work specifically for you because you will understand what each piece is doing. Combining those pieces into outfits then becomes so much easier. The process will become second nature.

Finding Your Balance

As we get into these details—textures, fabrics, colors, and so on—I don't want to lose sight of the end goal. All of this will help you build a wardrobe you love and put together outfits that make you feel your best. And the better you understand these technicalities, the easier that will be to do—and the greater freedom and flexibility you will have as a result. You will be able to take any look and adapt it effectively to your likes and lifestyle—something we talk about more in chapter 6.

Every piece of clothing you wear does something. The question is, is it working for you—for your style preferences and goals? Understanding the Style Formula, from cuts to colors, will help you figure that out, simplifying it to a science. You will then have the ability to be creatively inspired in a way that works for you.

In this chapter, we have talked about the many ways you can manipulate visual interest, including the use of color. The next question is, what colors are you using? Even with the perfect cut, fabric, and texture, a color that clashes with your natural tones can feel out of sync. Knowing your personal palette and how it interacts with your skin tone—and enhances your wardrobe—is just as important as knowing your body architecture.

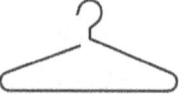

To the Closet: See Like a Stylist

To start fine-tuning your self-styling skills, it's helpful to get a sense of how individual pieces influence visual weight and affect where your eye lands. This affects your visual proportions by directing attention to specific areas, so it's useful to understand how it works. These exercises can help.

Exercise 1: Noticing Where Your Eye Lands

Head to your closet and select your brightest pair of pants or your brightest top. Pair it with something that is more muted. Look in the mirror and notice where the eye goes first. Now, try this: pair that same bright piece with something that has a pattern, texture, or shine to it—say, a silk blouse or a tweed jacket. It does not matter if the items match. This is just about putting things together, looking in the mirror, and seeing where your eye lands at first glance.

You can also try this with colors that seem "plain," like an optic white T-shirt. Pair this plain item with a dark piece and then step in front of the mirror. Where does your eye go? It is likely that your gaze gravitates to the white item. Simple as it is, it creates visual weight.

If you have trouble with this exercise standing in front of a mirror, you can also take photos of yourself in the various combinations. Looking at a picture on your screen may be an easier way to see it.

Exercise 2: Experimenting with Necklines

Color is just one of the components we've discussed in this chapter. You can also experience the power of cut by replicating the exercise I did with Maria and her boatneck top. Go to the closet and grab your favorite shirt. Notice what kind of neckline it has. V-neck? Crew neck? Boatneck? Put it on and stand in front of the mirror. Now manipulate the shirt to create alternative necklines. What differences do you notice?

Alternatively, if you own shirts with different necklines, try them on in secession and take photos of yourself in each one. Notice how the necklines change the look of your neck, shoulders, and bust, resulting in different types of visual weight—and then notice how the visual weight up top impacts the visual weight on the bottom half of the body. Visually changing the neckline can alter the overall silhouette. Do you have a preference in neckline?

All of this is to train your eye and deepen your understanding of how different clothes impact the balance of your look. You are seeing the clothes objectively, as a means of manipulating balance and impacting the overall presentation of an outfit. In short, you are starting to see like a stylist.

Unlock more style insights! Scan the QR code for exclusive content and interactive exercises to deepen your understanding of the chapter's key concepts and help you further explore your Style ID.

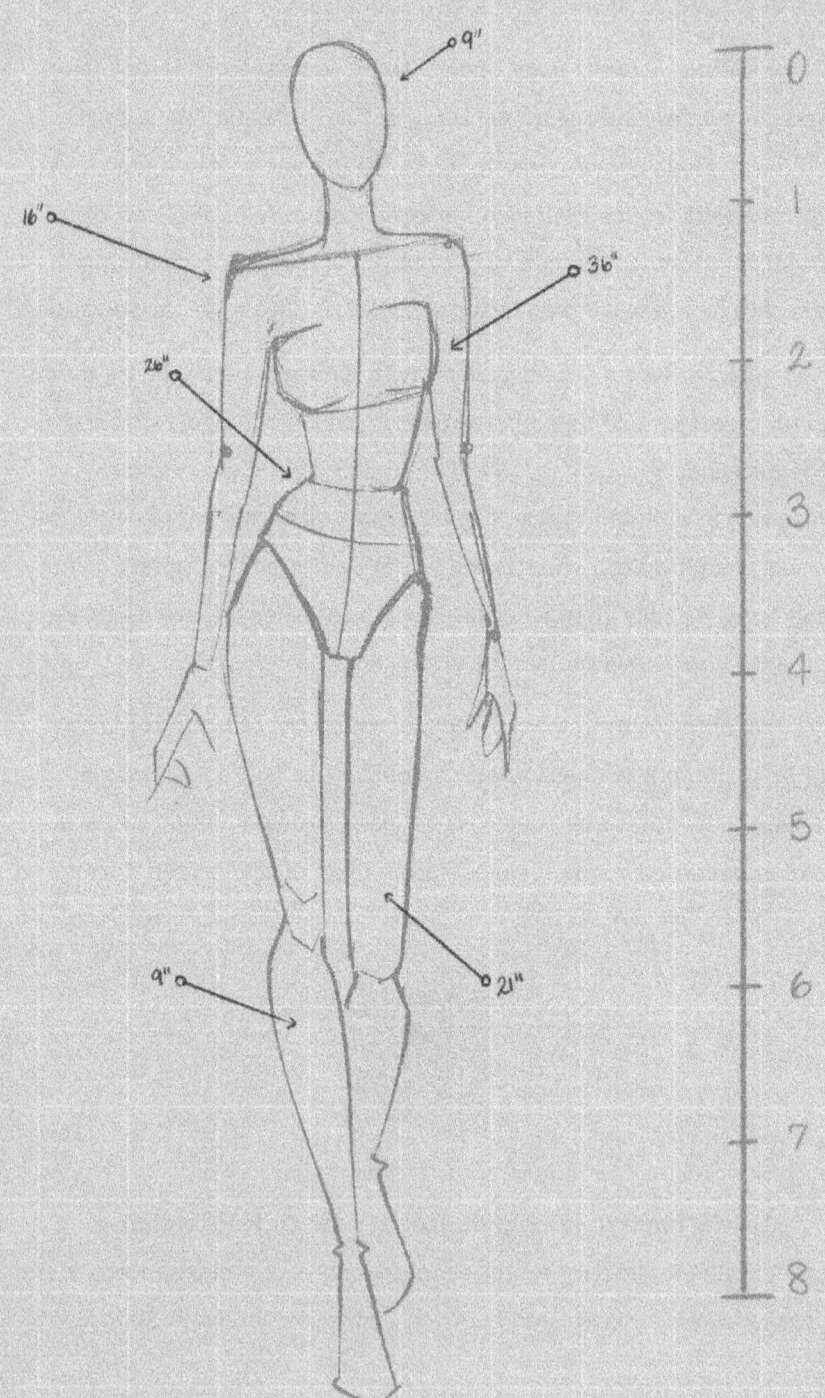

CHAPTER 5

Learning Your Color Science

I often give seminars on styling. From companies to women's groups, various organizations hire me to speak to their audience about how to dress effortlessly for any occasion. One of the most powerful tools for achieving this is understanding color—specifically how it can enhance your wardrobe, make getting dressed easier, and give you that natural glow.

During one seminar when I asked for questions, one woman's hand popped up immediately. Angela wanted to tell me about this jacket she had bought recently: "I went to the store, and there was this gorgeous leather jacket. It was amazing material, buttery soft, and it had this really cool big collar, and it fit perfectly. But it only came in one color. Burnt rose."

"When I put the jacket on, I could see that it wasn't the right color for me. But I loved it so much! So I got it." Then, she revealed, "But I almost never wear it, because I feel like it washes me out."

She explained that it was spending a lot of time in her closet because every time she tried to wear it, it just didn't seem to go with anything. Inevitably, she would end up taking it off and selecting something else. Having just heard the presentation, she had an insight: "Maybe I could wear a shawl over the jacket, so I'd have a different color right by my face, and then the jacket won't wash me out." I agreed that would prevent the washed-out look; however, the shawl would then be covering up that gorgeous jacket—what was supposed to be a key piece she could throw on and pair with a lot of items.

Angela's story highlights a common experience: falling in love with a piece that's almost perfect except for one key detail—in this case, its color. We've all done it. We get swept up in a fun cut, great fabric, or cool brand and convince ourselves we can make it work. But in the end, we find that one missing element, like the wrong color, is simply too hard to work around—and enough to keep us from reaching for that item.

In Angela's case, understanding her color science could have made all the difference. Understanding your personal coloring and choosing shades that complement it is one of the most transformative tools you can use in building a wardrobe that works for you. The good news is that everyone can wear any color—it's simply a matter of finding the right tone, shade, and intensity to match your unique coloring.

What Is Color Science?

Color science is the study of how your natural coloring—composed of your skin, hair, and eyes—interacts with the different colors you wear. This natural coloring is defined by the contrast between these features and how they complement each other. At Unfoldid, we use color science to determine your personal color palette, a grouping of specific colors that work with your coloring, also referred to as your "color season." Understanding your unique palette helps you choose clothing that enhances your appearance by aligning with your natural tones and contrast. By using color science, you can bring out the best in your skin, eyes, and hair, making your overall look more cohesive and polished.

We have talked about color in the previous chapters—but in those cases, we focused on the placement of color on the body, as a means of adding or subtracting visual interest. Now, we are talking about discovering which colors are complementary to your natural coloring. Understanding your color science is just as important as understanding your body architecture when it comes to choosing clothes and putting together outfits. You can manipulate the balance of your appearance by understanding your horizontal and vertical proportions. You can add a *glow* to your appearance by enhancing your natural coloring with your seasonal color palette, making your eyes "pop" and your skin luminous.

Building a Wardrobe with Color Science

Your personal color palette isn't just about wearing flattering colors—it's also a practical tool for building a functional wardrobe. When you know which shades complement you, shopping becomes easier, and your wardrobe becomes more cohesive. No more tops that wash you out or confusion about what colors go together. This will save time and money while eliminating the frustration of items that don't mix, and it will ensure you feel confident in everything you wear.

With a palette-based wardrobe, you'll find that most of your closet will mix and match easily. This is because colors within the same palette naturally complement one another. For example, a pair of chocolate-brown pants from your palette might pair effortlessly with an olive-green T-shirt or an eggplant-purple sweater. These items create multiple outfit options with fewer pieces.

And if you decide to introduce a bold color outside your palette—like a bright pink—you'll already know that it will likely be more of a specialty piece rather than a wardrobe staple. This knowledge helps you make smarter shopping decisions, ensuring that you only invest in items that work well with your existing wardrobe.

I see confusion around color with my clients all the time. Some people avoid it entirely, sticking to safe neutrals because they're unsure what colors suit them. Others embrace a variety of colors without considering whether those colors complement their natural coloring. In both cases, their wardrobes can feel disjointed or lacking in harmony. Once you know your personal palette, these challenges disappear, and you can build a wardrobe that always feels polished and versatile—and works for you.

Don't worry—your favorite colors aren't off-limits. One of the most freeing aspects of understanding your color science is realizing that once you identify your palette, you can wear any color. Ah … I can almost hear the sigh of relief! It's just about choosing the version of that color that works for you.

Take red, for example. There is brick red, primary red, fire-engine red, crimson, scarlet, garnet, cherry, rose…. Of all the reds out there, there *is* one that works for your palette. And your color palette will help you determine which one it is.

Knowing your palette will make dressing easier in a few ways, as it can help you:

- **Easily pick pieces that give you a glow.** Certain colors blend with your natural coloring and make you luminous. They might make your cheeks look richer or make your face look brighter. Other colors do not blend with your natural coloring

- **Build a wardrobe that's workable.** Color science creates a concrete blueprint you can use to build a cohesive wardrobe that mixes and matches easily, making outfit creation a breeze. Because when you build a wardrobe from your palette, all your colors will work together. Shopping is also easier, because you will know what colors work, and new pieces will pair easily with the items already in your wardrobe, saving time and money.

- **Stay true to your preferences.** Knowing your color palette also allows you to wear the colors you naturally gravitate toward by showing you which version complements you. Love orange? Your color palette tells you exactly which type of orange will suit you.

Identifying Your Palette

The idea of color science is sometimes presented as "seasons." The concept of color seasons, popularized in *Color Me Beautiful* by Carole Jackson, is still widely used today, though it has evolved over time. In Jackson's system, people are divided into four seasons—spring, summer, autumn, and winter—based on their natural coloring:

- **Spring:** bright, warm hues with yellow undertones
- **Summer:** cool, soft colors with blue undertones
- **Autumn:** deep, earthy colors with orange or gold undertones
- **Winter:** cool, clear colors with blue undertones

We use the expanded concept of color seasons at Unfoldid, breaking down the four seasons into more precise categories according to how strong, true, or muted they are. This ensures that your palette perfectly complements your natural coloring and helps you make more informed wardrobe choices.

A color analysis helps identify your seasonal color palette and is an important part of our process using the Style Formula at Unfoldid. This is defined by three primary characteristics: skin undertone (warm, cool), contrast level (high, medium, low), and the depth of your features (light, medium, dark). The goal is to echo these elements of your natural coloring in your seasonal color palette. Each of these three elements—undertone, contrast, and depth—is incorporated into your seasonal palette, making it easy to use when shopping and building a wardrobe.

Just like you only have to learn your body's architecture once, coloring also tends to remain consistent until much later in life. And once you learn your color palette, you don't need to worry about anyone else's—you can focus on understanding and using *your* colors to their fullest. The science is here to give you objectivity, so you can discover what colors make you glow.

At Unfoldid, we combine several methods and apply a trained eye to quickly and accurately identify all the elements of your natural coloring. Here, I'll provide an overview of our favorite methods for determining the three elements of your seasonal color palette—undertone, contrast, and depth. The exercises at the end of the chapter will guide you through our favorites including determining the most essential element: whether you have warm or cool undertones.

UNDERTONE

Identifying your undertone or color temperature is the first and most important step in identifying your color palette, since every palette falls into a primary category of warm or cool. Whether your skin is light or dark, it has a natural undertone that leans either warm (golden, peachy, or yellow) or cool (bluish, pinkish, or reddish). This distinction is integral because it lays the foundation for your color season.

For example, if you have warm undertones, you'll likely look best in warm shades like pumpkin-spice orange or golden olive—colors that look more brown, as if they have been "toasted"—rather than primary orange or green. If your undertones are cool, colors like icy blue or raspberry will enhance your features, as these colors both have cooler undertones of blue or green and lack the "toasted" warmth of yellow or brown.

DEPTH

The next step is to determine your depth, or how light or dark your overall coloring is. Assess the hair, skin, and eyes including details like the eyebrows, lips, iris, and other elements. Some people have an overall lightness to all these features. Others fall in the middle and have medium depth, because their features fall into the midrange for hair, skin, and eyes. Though they may have some light features, most are medium in depth, with almost no dark features. Someone considered deep would have overall depth to all the features of their hair, skin, and eyes or have very dominant dark features. So someone with lighter skin but with many dark or very prominent deep features would still be considered deep.

Determining your overall depth determines the depth of color that will enhance but not overpower your natural coloring. In general, people with lighter coloring look best in lighter colors while those with deeper coloring can wear deeper colors well.

CONTRAST

The last step is to assess your contrast level, or the difference in lightness and darkness between your features, eyes, skin, and hair and other details like eyebrows and iris. For example, someone with light skin and dark hair has higher contrast, while someone with fair skin and light eyes has lower contrast. And someone with darker skin with bright, golden eyes may have medium contrast, while someone with dark skin and very dark eyes would be considered low contrast.

People with high contrast tend to look best in bright, saturated colors, while those with low contrast tend to look best in soft or more muted colors. Knowing your level of contrast helps you understand whether you will favor those softer, more washed-out colors or bright, high-intensity colors. Again, there is an exercise to help you determine your contrast at the chapter's end.

PUTTING IT TOGETHER

Each of the twelve seasonal palettes is a distinct combination of the three elements of undertone, depth, and contrast.

CHAPTER 5

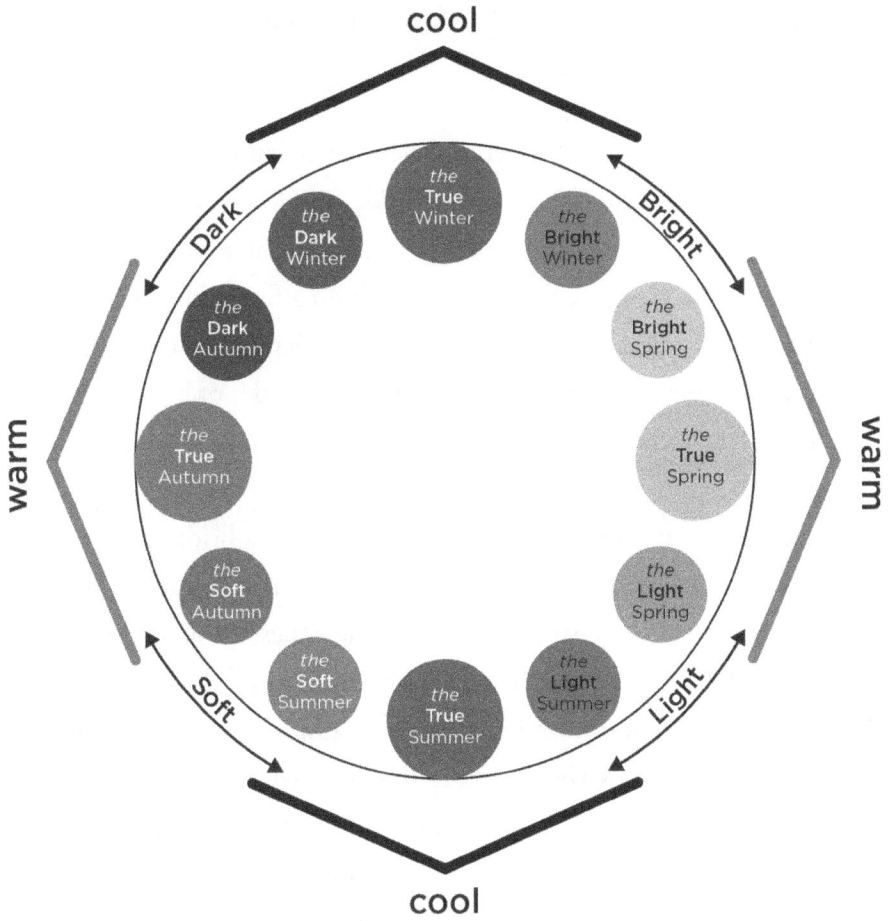

How the color seasons break down in terms of undertone, depth, and contrast

After you have determined these three elements, you only need to match these to the color seasons wheel. It is then a process of elimination. For example, once you are sure you are warm, you have eliminated half of the choices; next, look at depth and contrast, whichever you are most confident in, to narrow it down to your seasonal palette.

Applying Your Understanding of Color to What You Wear

Once you have your seasonal color palette, you will know what colors suit you best. By unlocking a deeper understanding of color, you can open more possibilities for yourself. You will be able to wear almost any color you want, because you'll be able to find modified colors based on their characteristics, like undertone, depth, and contrast. To understand how that's possible, it helps to get an idea of how clothing color differs according to the characteristics of undertone, contrast, and depth.

Let's start with undertone. If you walk into a bridal store, you will see dresses in many different whites. Pearl. Cream. Eggshell. Ivory. An actual optic white has cool undertones and is found only in cool palettes, while people with warm undertones glow more with a cream, with its warm undertones, for example. Determining your color palette ensures you have the "color of white" that works for you—any of the whites named above, from pearl to a deep cream, will present as white in your wardrobe. You want to use the "white" from your palette that enhances your unique coloring.

Now, let's look at soft to bright (which is determined by your contrast). Take red. The truth is, not all red is the same. Think of when you buy a brand-new red T-shirt. It's probably very bright. However, when you put that red T-shirt through the wash twenty times, it fades, becoming more muted or soft. It's still red, but less intense. For people with low contrast, that faded red is a better fit than a bold, bright version.

Next, we have an example of light to dark, which is determined by your depth. Consider a kelly green. It is vivid and rich. If you add white to it, it becomes lighter and lighter, turning pastel green. The lighter you are, the lighter are the colors that work with your natural coloring. If you are darker, then deeper, richer colors work best.

Your personal palette takes all of these elements into account and provides you with a set of colors in the spectrum of warm to cool, soft to bright, and light to dark that work for you. This deeper understanding helps you to identify those colors and expand your palette.

When talking about color with my clients, I try to avoid technical terms—what I call the "artist names" for characteristics of color. That said, I think an overview can be useful:

- **Hue:** The specific name of the color, such as brick red versus fire-engine red, or olive green versus forest green. Hue refers to the exact position on the color wheel and is the primary factor in determining if a color is warm or cool.

- **Value:** How light or dark a color is, with pure white being very light and pure black being very dark. Value is the primary factor that determines the depth of a color.

- **Chroma:** The purity, intensity, or saturation of a color, with high chroma colors, like electric blue, indicating bright, saturated colors and low chroma colors, like misty blue, being more muted. Chroma correlates with contrast, which indicates the saturation of a color.

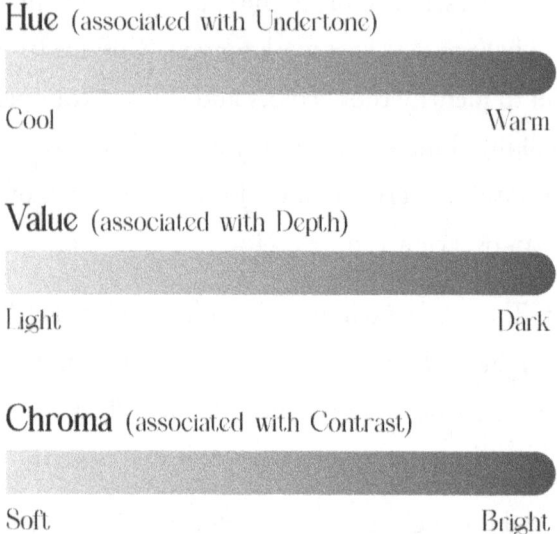

Each of these three qualities of color exists on a spectrum

When people say something like, "I can't wear green; it's a bad color on me," what they are really saying is that they can't wear a certain hue, value, or chroma of green. The undertone or the value or the chroma is not working for them. Consider the difference between a bright, primary green, an olive green, and a kelly green, for example. The olive green looks like it has a hint of brown in it; it's like a toasted version of primary green, appearing warmer as a result. Meanwhile, the kelly green looks like it has a blue tinge to it, making it appear cooler as a result. In our world of styling, that olive green may be the answer to the client who says, "I can't wear green."

Any color can be warm or cool, bright or muted, dark or light. If you are a true winter, for example, you have cool coloring. It's bright and defined, not soft and muted. The colors that suit you tend to be vibrant. For example, a burnt rose will not suit a true winter. Instead, you might look for more saturated, bright versions of the shade, like raspberry.

All these different elements of a color are what make it work for you (or not). Your personal seasonal palette takes each of these into account to provide a curated set of shades unique to your Style ID. We then offer this deeper understanding of color to empower you to identify and even expand your palette, enhancing your style with confidence.

By determining your seasonal palette, you now have identified the colors of the color wheel for your unique Style ID. By understanding more about how color works, you can wear almost any color, as long as you adapt it to your season. Finally, if you struggle to recognize colors or have any level of color blindness, there are apps available to assist in identifying colors.

You can also strategically incorporate colors outside your season by wearing them away from your face or mixing and matching them with neutrals. For instance, if you love a vibrant purple but it's not in your season, try it as an accent piece—like a belt, bag, or shoes—rather than as a top or dress. In fact, knowing your palette allows you to add fun pieces that are completely outside your palette thoughtfully and with intention, understanding they will not be as versatile or easy to mix and match as pieces within your palette.

Making Color Work for You

Once you know your color palette, you can dress more easily for every day. For example, all of my gym clothes are in colors that are true to my color science. When I go to the gym, I'm usually rolling out of bed. I don't put on a full face of makeup or do my hair. Knowing that I am wearing a color that suits me and does not wash me out allows me to get in my workout while feeling good doing it. I can step out the door without any stress or hassle.

Understanding color science also makes it easier to dress for special occasions. Take the idea of the little black dress (LBD), a wardrobe staple that many people have in their closet. If black is not in your seasonal palette, then the LBD in your wardrobe may not be black. For example, black is not in my personal palette. Instead, I opt for a lot of charcoal grays. So my LBD is actually an LGD, or little gray dress. Another person might have an LND, or little navy dress.

Color should also work for your lifestyle—something we'll talk about more in the next chapter. Say you're a mom of a toddler, and you spend most days playing with your child, going to the park, preparing food, and tackling all kinds of hands-on activities. Lighter colors might not be the most practical choice when you're sitting in the grass or making mud pies with your little one. A wardrobe built around darker colors in easy-care, wrinkle-free fabrics may make more sense for you—at least until the kids are older.

This practical approach to color is a key part of the Style Formula, which starts with understanding your body architecture, your horizontal proportions, and your vertical proportions, followed by your color science. The result of color science determines what colors, including their value and chroma, work best for you based upon your skin tone, eyes, and hair color. The next component of the Style Formula? Your likes and lifestyle.

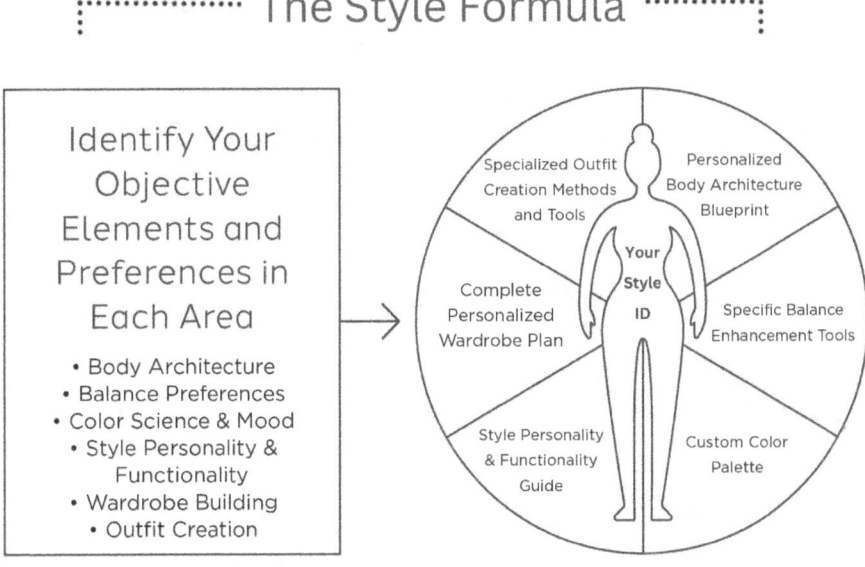

A refresh of what the Style Formula looks like

In the next chapter, we're going to look at how your personal style preferences and lifestyle factor into your Style ID, exploring how to align your wardrobe with what you love and how you live, empowering you to dress with confidence and ease.

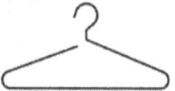

To the Closet: Find Your Glow

There are a few fast-track tools you can use to begin understanding your color science. These exercises are a starting point. Try them in natural light without any makeup.

Exercises for Identifying Undertone

Identifying the undertones (warm or cool) of your coloring is the first step to determining your season. One way to figure this out is to put on a true white T-shirt or hold a sheet of white paper next to your face or by the neck and chest. Now, look closely and notice how your skin reacts. If it appears more pink, rosy, or blue-purple, you have cool undertones. If it appears more peachy, yellow, or golden, you have warm undertones.

Your natural hair color can be another good indicator of your color temperature. Even though hair color can change over time—whether naturally or through dyeing—the undertones remain consistent and can guide your palette. Look closely at your hairline at the base of the neck. Are there warm hints such as red, auburn, or gold? Or do you instead notice hints of cool, more ashy gray colors or stark white—or for darker hair, blue or violet?

Many have also heard of the vein test for undertones. If you can see your veins on the inside of your wrist, greenish veins suggest warm undertones, while people with blue or purplish-looking veins usually have cooler undertones. You can also look around the gums for hints of blue or purple, indicating cool undertones, or more peachy undertones, indicating warm.

Your eye color can also offer clues about your seasonal color palette. Cool undertones are often paired with icy blue, gray, or cool brown eyes, while warm undertones may come with golden brown, hazel with gold flecks, or softer blues and greens.

Each person finds different methods easier when distinguishing their coloring. I find the color comparison test to be the simplest. It's all about observing how your skin reacts when placed next to different colors.

Start by testing fabric or clothing in distinctly warm colors (like mustard, peach, honey browns, olive green, burnt orange) and distinctly cool colors (like baby blue, icy pink, magenta, emerald). Notice how your skin reacts: Which colors make your skin look vibrant, bright, or smooth? Which ones wash you out or emphasize unevenness or create shadows? Next, try pulling pieces from your own closet that you instinctively feel work, and those you think do not, and again observe how your skin reacts. By observing these differences, you can determine your undertone and the colors that complement it.

Exercises for Understanding Depth

One of the simplest ways to determine your depth is to take a photo of your face with your hair showing and turn it into 100 percent grayscale, removing all the color. If your depth is light, the overall image will be light. Medium depth might show some light parts and others darker. Deep depth will have some deep, dominant features standing out. For example, the eyes or hair could stand out as very dark compared to the face.

Another method to determine your depth is by assigning values to your hair, skin, eyes, and mouth. For example, a value of one is light, two is medium, and three is dark. If you have mostly ones, you are light. If you have mostly twos, you are medium. Mostly threes means dark. The method creates some objectivity and separation in seeing our features.

Exercises for Understanding Contrast

We can revisit the two methods used for depth above as a way to measure your natural contrast. Again, assign values of one, two, and three to your hair, skin, eyes, and mouth. If you have mostly one number, you have low contrast. If you have only ones and threes, you have high contrast. Again, a black-and-white photo will make contrasts in your features more prominent, so it's easier to see and determine your contrast.

Now reference the seasons graphic earlier in the chapter—if you feel very confident about any of the three elements, begin the process of elimination to narrow down your specific seasonal palette.

The Colors in Your Closet Exercise

Finally, one of the easiest ways to figure out a person's palette has been, in my experience, by simply looking in their closet. A lot of people have a sense of what colors give them that glow and will purposefully buy items in that color, even if they are not consciously sticking to their palette.

You probably already have an idea of what colors make you light up. Let's take a look at them now. Go to your closet and take a look at the colors you have hanging there. Do you have almost no color—say, a lot of black, gray, or white? Do you have every color of the rainbow—does it look like a box of crayons?

Look for repetition in your closet, colors that pop up again and again. Often, when I'm styling clients and visit their closet, I notice they tend to gravitate toward one or two colors from their palette, buying numerous items in those particular colors because they've realized they like how they look in them.

When you notice a repetition like that—or maybe it's not a repetition but you have a piece of clothing that you know makes you glow—take a piece of clothing in that color out of your closet and put it on.

Now, check.... Do your cheeks have a hint of color? Do your eyes sparkle? Is your skin shimmering? Or have the colors on your face become less pronounced and more washed out? Are there suddenly shadows near the corner or under your eyes? Do your eyes themselves look less sparkling and pronounced? Are there more shadows now between the chin and neck? Take a photo of yourself in that item.

Next, do you have anything that you rarely wear, because you feel like it's not a great color for you? Maybe it's something that washes you out or does not pair well with the rest of your wardrobe. You put it on and just know something is not quite right. Think of Angela and her rose jacket from the top of this chapter. Try on that item.

Again, look in the mirror and check. Is that glow in action—or not? Take a photo of yourself in that item too.

Save those two photos to help guide you as you unlock your color science. They are a testament to the difference that color can make, either washing you out or making you shine a bit brighter. That is the power of color science.

Unlock more style insights! Scan the QR code for exclusive content and interactive exercises to deepen your understanding of the chapter's key concepts and help you further explore your Style ID.

CHAPTER 6

Reflecting Your Likes and Lifestyle

"I've never really had a personal style; I just go with whatever's in stores." This is something I hear from so many clients. But the truth is, we all have a personal style. We all have some inkling of what we like and don't like, what resonates with us and what does not, and what feels true to our authentic self. It's that style intuition we talked about in chapter 2, that spark of attraction when you see a certain piece. That spark is what makes you feel happy when you slip on your coziest sweater or favorite jeans. If it's missing, you probably will not feel your best in what you are wearing.

This was the case for a client of mine—I'll call her Tara—who was preparing for her first serious job out of college. She was twenty-five and worried about looking too young or inexperienced, so she had invested in a few traditional Brooks Brothers pantsuits. However, she wasn't happy with the way they looked on her—they fit her body architecture, but something was not quite right. That's when she came to me.

The pantsuits Tara had chosen were in line with parts of her Style ID, as they fit well and worked with her proportions, and the colors complemented her skin tone. The suits also complied with the company dress policy. But there was one problem—she really didn't like them. She had become so caught up in wanting to appear professional in her new role, she'd dressed for the office without any regard for her own likes. Her new, professional outfits didn't reflect her authentic self, which left her feeling uncomfortable and drained her confidence. It wasn't just that she didn't like the way the clothes looked on her; she didn't feel good in them because they didn't allow her to express who she was. The pantsuits felt almost like a costume—stiff, formal, and the opposite of who she was as a person.

As we zeroed in on Tara's style, we helped her find ways to harness it in a way that worked for her—and made her happy with what she was wearing. We were able to mix in pieces from her original wardrobe that better reflected her authentic personal style, while incorporating her love of color and her sporty inclination to create perfectly professional looks that felt like *her*. We also looked at other brands beyond Brooks Brothers to find options that better fit her tastes.

There are so many different ways to express authenticity in a pantsuit or wear it in a unique way. If you give ten different people the same pantsuit, there is a way to style it for each one in a way that reflects their unique preferences and makes it their own. It could be through the accessories they choose, for example, or the blouse and shoes they pair with it. You can bring a part of yourself to any outfit you put together—but first you have to know your personal style preferences.

Personal style is an expression of your authentic self, and it's entirely unique to you. When you are in tune with it, the external influences we talked about in chapter 2 become less dominant, allowing your individual taste to shine. Your style is a reflection of your personal brand—like a signature. It's the reason two people will make the same pair of jeans look completely different—each one applies their unique preferences. Being able to articulate your style preferences helps you to pick pieces you feel good in and shop with a keen eye, building a cohesive wardrobe that is distinctly yours. This foundation then lets you put those pieces together effortlessly in a way that reflects your true self.

Our clothing tells the story of us. If you have things in your closet that you are not happy with or that don't speak to you, it is probably because they don't align with your authentic personal style. By taking time to discover and refine your personal style, you create a guidebook and develop instincts regarding what you wear and how. You can then control the message your clothing is sending externally while empowering yourself internally. We feel most comfortable and confident when we are in clothes that reflect our authentic selves.

The red leather jacket anecdote is my favorite way to demonstrate this because I know I have felt this way and think it resonates with many of us. Say you see someone on social media in a bright-red leather jacket. This person looks amazing. Confident, stylish, and put together. That jacket conveys a message of self-assurance, and it carries an entire mood with it.

You order the jacket. It arrives, and you can't wait to try it on. But when you do, the effect just isn't the same. It fits you. The jacket itself looks like the image you saw and is obviously of nice quality. But why doesn't it look the same on you as it did on that person on social media? It's simply that this jacket isn't in line with your Style ID. Maybe the color is not right for your palette. Maybe the shiny leather adds visual weight to your upper half, when you'd prefer to create more balance by adding visual weight to your lower half. Or maybe the zippers on the shoulders attract attention to an area you'd rather downplay. Disappointed, you send the jacket back.

But there is no need for disappointment. Because that jacket still had something you wanted that is worth taking note of: a mood. It resonated with your authentic style personality. Your style intuition sat up and took notice. You thought, "Hey, I want that jacket." What you were really thinking was, "I want the effect of that jacket." It carried a visual impact that you hoped to replicate—and you still can. It just won't come in the form of that specific jacket.

And then the fun begins. You can get back to the technicalities and figure out how to capture the mood of that jacket while staying true to your Style ID. So maybe instead of a shiny, red leather, you opt for a matte maroon, with undertones of purple. Maybe instead of a slightly longer jacket that cuts in at the hip, you opt for a shorter jacket that hits higher on the hip, elongating your legs. Maybe that slightly shorter jacket has some big pockets that hit at your hip, adding more visual interest to the bottom.

In this way, you mimic the vibe of the original jacket you saw in a way that works with your own Style ID. That is how you will create the mood you want—not by simply getting the exact same jacket.

People often equate being stylish with being trendy. To me, almost the opposite is true. Being stylish is really about tapping into your own authenticity—what you love, what makes you uniquely you—and embracing what resonates on a personal level. Equipped with that knowledge, you will understand how to adapt trends to your clothing preferences and lifestyle, instead of trying to mold yourself to trends.

It's time to find a style that's true to your authentic self—and that works for your real-world, everyday life, whether that's wrangling toddlers, giving board presentations, grabbing drinks with friends, hitting the hiking trails, or, depending on the day of the week, all of the above.

CHAPTER 6

Developing a Style That's True to You

Exploring and developing your own style starts with simply paying close attention to what you like and what you are naturally drawn to. It is likely that this is something you are doing subconsciously but haven't had the time or inclination or energy to focus on. With our busy lives, it is easy to fly right past these moments of recognition and continue on with our day-to-day obligations. Now, I am asking you to take just a moment to press pause and think about it.

Discovering your authentic personal style is a process of investigation, and no matter where you are in your journey, it's an important and fun part of creating your Style ID. This is not meant to be an instant makeover where you are suddenly dressing like a rockstar. It's also not a one-time event but a continual evolution. Your style is a reflection of your own likes and dislikes and also of the influences and experiences you have collected over the years. It's your story. Styles change, as do lifestyles, but when we have a good sense of our true preferences, we can adapt easily. By more clearly defining our personal style, we develop guidelines—a road map—that help us shop and build a cohesive wardrobe that reflects our authentic selves. With this approach, our style evolves naturally alongside the changes in our lives, continually refining itself to reflect who we are.

So, how am I going to help you uncover your authentic style—the look that makes you shine and feel your best? With a formula to help guide you through the process. Ultimately, the key to identifying your style is to explore. Look everywhere in your life. Keep your eyes and your mind open to things that appeal to you, without worrying about why. You can then identify patterns in what you like. Let's look at some of the best ways to begin your exploration process.

GO ON A STYLE INTUITION DISCOVERY TOUR: CREATING YOUR MOOD BOARD

Mood boards are an excellent way to identify patterns, which is the key to unlocking your authentic style. At the end of chapter 2, I asked you to get in touch with your style intuition by pinpointing items in your wardrobe (or in a store) that you simply love, no explanation needed, and taking photos of them. This was your first step to discovering your authentic style and the start of the mood board process.

Find a broader selection of items to add to your mood board by exploring blogs, social media, magazines, and more. You could even hit the shops. No, you're not actually going shopping—this is just a discovery tour. Take pictures of items you love, even if you are not sure why. The end-of-chapter exercise has some more guidance for mood boarding and analyzing what you find. Here, we outline several other ways to explore and discover what you love to add more inspiration to your mood board.

PICK YOUR FAVORITES

Odds are that if I asked you to pick your three favorite pieces, you could walk to your closet and pull them out immediately. Don't think about the occasion or the season. Whether it's your favorite winter coat or a pair of high heels you wish you could wear every day, or your favorite tee, these are your go-to pieces that you know always "work" and make you feel great.

More broadly, think about your favorite things. Do you love large earrings? Tropical patterns? A specific time in history like Victorian or mod? These are also a piece of your style and likely influence or are reflected in the way you dress. And this doesn't have to apply to clothing and accessories only. Hair and makeup tastes can also indicate your style. Maybe you prefer sleek hairstyles, like low-slung ponytails and chignons. Or maybe you prefer a wild mane of loose locks.

You can even look beyond fashion completely. Consider interior design. Whether you live in a cozy studio or a spacious four-bedroom home, your space likely reflects a sense of style in how you choose to decorate. Do you like oversized, plush furniture? Do you prefer minimalist, Scandinavian-inspired pieces? Is a fluffy area rug your thing, or do you prefer bare hardwood floors? When you picked your kitchen backsplash, did you opt for something plain in a muted hue or colorful tiles? Look at interior design catalogs and social media feeds. Whichever route you take, it can be helpful to take it out of context from clothing, precisely because our relationships to clothing can be so personal and complicated. These details give you a peek at your personal style.

STUDY YOUR FASHION HEROES

Look at the people around you, both fictional and real world. Do you have a fashion hero? It could be an influencer. It could be a Hollywood star. It could be a character in a show. It does not matter if they look like you or share your body architecture or palette or anything else. It's just someone who you consider fashionable. Every time you see them, you think, "Gosh, I love their style." That could well be one of your fashion heroes.

Search online for images of that person and look for patterns in what they wear. Maybe it's a movie star who wears a lot of voluminous ball gowns on the red carpet and frilly summer dresses in everyday life. Or maybe it's a TV character known for his sharply cut suits and matching cufflinks. Or maybe it's an influencer with a bit of a boho vibe, often wearing flowing skirts and oversized earrings. Whoever your fashion hero is, collect images of them in outfits you love.

CREATE AN ANTIMOOD BOARD

Figuring out what you like is just as much a matter of figuring out what you don't like. Often, this is the easy part! You can make an antimood board if you like, using the various steps above. Highlight all the things that make you say, "Thanks, but not for me." My antimood board would include everything from flouncy baby-pink dresses to frilly white-lace bedspreads—all things that just feel overly delicate and dainty for my personal style.

All of these things that you are drawn to visually point toward your natural style inclinations. Identifying patterns across these various areas, whether it's your own wardrobe or interior design elements or historical eras, will help you get in touch with that personal style. We will explore this more in the exercise at the end of the chapter.

As you develop a clearer sense of your personal style, coupled with other elements of your Style ID, you'll be able to adapt it to any occasion—even something as big as the Grammy Awards. My client Susan Leger-Ferraro knows from experience!

A Testament to the Power of Styling: Susan Leger-Ferraro, Humanitarian, Author, Entrepreneur

Susan is a social entrepreneur and sought-after business innovator who launched her first multi-million-dollar business when she was just a teenager. She is a champion of women's empowerment and diversity causes—and the wonderful work she does led to an unexpected invitation: to the 2024 Grammy Awards! I had the opportunity to help her get ready for the amazing moment.

CHAPTER 6

I am passionate about supporting diversity in business and have spearheaded multiple initiatives toward that end. One of the more recent companies I launched empowered African artists to shift generational poverty to generational wealth through artist education, focusing primarily on publishing and copyright advisory services. Coincidentally, the 2024 Grammys saw the debut of the Best African Music Performance category—and I had the good fortune to be invited by some of the artists I'd worked with through the company.

The invite was unexpected and last minute, so I was texting Aricia just two weeks before the event for help on what to wear. Despite the time crunch, she managed to connect me with two amazing African designers, and I ended up with three gorgeous outfits for the event. We were all elated by the end result—it was a global celebration!

I always tell Aricia that she is not just a stylist or a fashion buyer, but an image consultant. She pays attention to how *you* want to show up in the world and helps you understand how to achieve that goal, while also helping you understand how the choices you make may be perceived. She integrates pieces of your own vibe while ensuring you are showing up in a way that meets the conventions of the context, whether it's a corporate meeting or an awards show.

I'm all for being a rebel. However, over the course of my career, I've learned that there are moments where you need to meet people where they are at, and first build trust and respect in order to collaborate effectively—especially when it comes to moving forward social issues. Despite how far we've come with the feminist movement, women in particular still face so much pressure and judgment regarding how they look. That's just a fact. Plus, research tells us that first impressions happen in mere seconds, making that initial moment of visual impact even more critically important.

Whether male, female, or nonbinary, Aricia's clients learn how to present themselves in a way that aligns with the true spirit of who they are, while also projecting the image they want the world to see. By understanding the significance of their styling choices, people from all walks of life can engage with whatever opportunity comes their way—even a once-in-a-lifetime event like the Grammys.

Reflecting Your Unique Lifestyle

Your likes are not the only consideration in defining your personal style. There is also your life to think about. Your authentic style needs to fit your lifestyle. It needs to be functional. And it needs to be current to your time and place. The story of my client, Lilly, can help demonstrate what I mean.

Lilly was a professional woman stepping into a new chapter of her life with a fresh degree and a new job. She worked in finance with high-net-worth clients and had to look polished and put together at work. She also had to be ready for school pickups and playdates in the park. When Lilly came to me, she expressed a desire to update her look for both facets of her busy lifestyle—without hassle.

Lilly was already in tune with her personal style, which leaned toward a classic look. Sharply tailored suits, muted hues, and simple and sleek accessories were her go-to items. Her issue was how to take her classic style and make it more adaptable, so she could take it from boardrooms to baby care.

One of the easiest and quickest things we could do to transition her wardrobe was to mix and match her usual work suits, creating more versatile combinations suited to each part of her day. So instead of wearing the usual matching pants, jacket, and blouse underneath, she wore a simple crew neck T-shirt. Imagine the difference: the matching jacket and blouse are ideal for a high-profile meeting, but swapping in a fitted T-shirt made the same tailored pieces feel relaxed enough for school pickup or a walk through the park, while still looking polished. This simple change allowed Lilly to embrace her classic style without compromising comfort or ease for her new lifestyle.

To complete her wardrobe, we shopped for practical pieces that could withstand the busy mom life and still work in the office. A sleek pair of sneakers could be worn when chasing after the kids or to work, for example. We also considered fabrics, focusing on dark hues that hid stains easily and washable materials that didn't require dry-cleaning. We introduced a few elevated basics that could seamlessly transition between her two worlds, like softer knit blazers in modern stretch fabrics. These pieces kept her looking polished for client meetings while feeling comfortable and flexible enough for sitting on the floor during playdates or dashing to school pickup. Bit by bit, we built a closet that fit her new, expanded life.

In order to build an ideal wardrobe for you, you also have to build a wardrobe that fits your lifestyle and environment. It needs to be functional, serving whatever occasions you encounter day to day. Whether it's dinner with your friends or playdates with your kids and their friends, everything you need will be hanging in your closet. Our goal is to build a wardrobe that matches your lifestyle, proportionate to how much time you spend on those activities. So if you go to the gym three days a week and only need business attire four times a year for quarterly meetings, you will have more gym clothes than business attire in your closet. If you take the kids to the playground every Tuesday and Thursday afternoon, and dress up for a fancy night out only once a month, you will have considerably more comfort-casual clothes than evening wear.

I always work with my clients to come up with a rough percentage of how they spend their time and then create a pie chart to visually break it down. Do you spend most of your time in the office, or do you work from home and spend your time mainly in your own house? Do you spend most of your workweek traveling to business meetings, or are you pretty stationary? Do you spend most of your nights out on the town, or are you a homebody?

At the end of this chapter, I've included an exercise to help you make your own lifestyle pie chart. After you complete a closet edit, which we talk about in the next chapter, you can create a second pie chart that estimates what is actually currently in your wardrobe. Then we compare the two to see which areas are underrepresented, for example not enough practical comfort shoes, and areas that may be overrepresented—in my case, high heels that I love but hardly ever wear! This process helps you to more clearly see what you have and need, aiding you in both editing your closet and in creating a more targeted shopping list that will keep you on track building a cohesive wardrobe full of everything you need. We will talk about it more in the next chapter, which is all about building your wardrobe.

CHAPTER 6

My Lifestyle

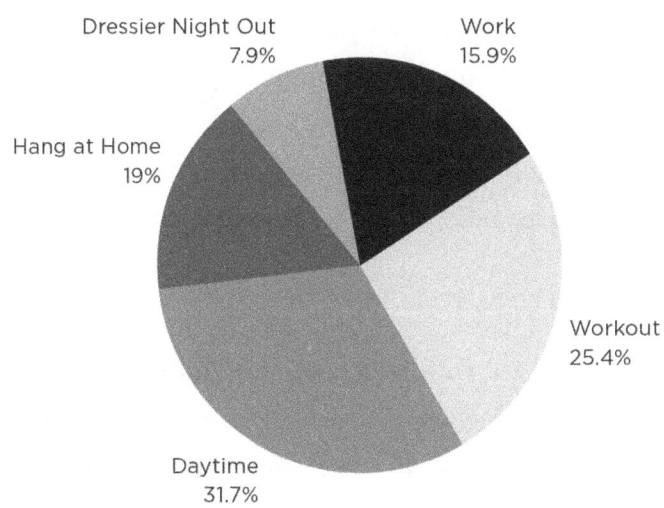

My Current Wardrobe

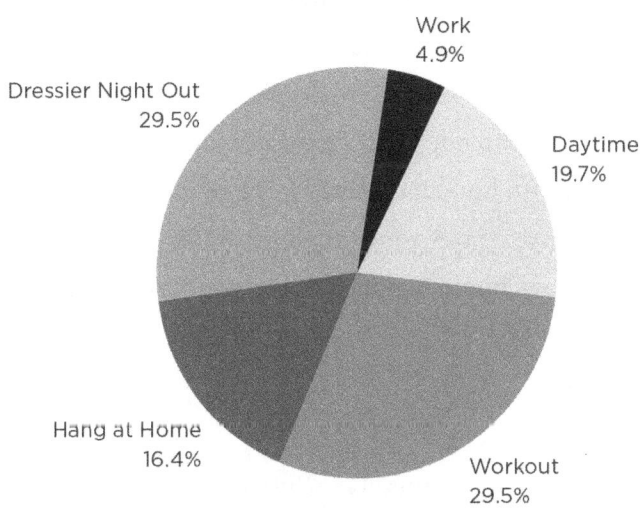

An example of lifestyle and wardrobe pie charts

With this, you can build a functional wardrobe—which will look different for different people. What is "functional" for you depends on all kinds of factors, from your job to your hobbies. The goal is to make it as easy as possible to dress for your days, however those are spent.

To ensure your wardrobe truly supports your lifestyle, it's helpful to identify the specific types of clothes you need for each activity while keeping a few additional considerations in mind. Though much of this may feel like common sense, it's helpful to have a guide.

SEASONS AND CLIMATE

If you live in a place with long summers and short, mild winters, you probably are not going to have a wardrobe packed with wooly sweaters and puffer jackets. Just like you probably won't have endless sundresses and shorts if you live in a place with harsh winters and cool summers. Temperature is only one factor to think about when building a climate-friendly wardrobe. How much rain does your area get? Lots of damp weather makes waterproof shoes a must. Does it tend to get windy? Outerwear that can cut that chilly breeze is a smart investment. Is there a lot of sun—do you need some awesome hats for protection? You do not need a separate wardrobe for every season. Rather, you want to build a core wardrobe of essential elements that will optimally serve you. A good starting point is asking yourself how many seasons your home region has. Do you have a distinct spring, summer, fall, and winter?

MAINTENANCE

Consider what level of maintenance fits your lifestyle or what level you are willing to take on. Fabrics and cleaning requirements are also something to think about. If you travel often or simply don't have time to iron, look for fabrics that fold well without wrinkles, so you can just grab them and go. Do you have the time and budget for a weekly trip to the dry cleaner, or would it be easier to have items that can all be thrown in the washing machine? We have so many choices these days in modern fabrics. Determine how much time and energy you have to care for your clothes, so that what you buy fits your needs.

DRESS CODES AND PRACTICALITIES

Sometimes, particular requirements influence what we wear. Are there any dress codes to consider, like no jeans at the office or a blazer required at certain meetings? Do you need to avoid scarves or loose clothing at your print shop or studio? If you're a mom with young children and you are out on the playground, that will influence your daily style choices and the wardrobe you put together. If you walk your dog on nature trails at lunch, dark-colored sneakers may be preferable to white. Depending on the type of physical activity, the cut of the clothing matters too. Say you bike to work every day. You may want a work wardrobe centered around pants, instead of skirts, or flats instead of heels.

COMFORT

When you make your lifestyle pie chart at the chapter's conclusion, consider things like how much walking you will be doing in each "slice" of the pie. Are you walking and taking the subway to work? Or is it a fancy dinner where you will valet? Are you going dancing after? With all the new developments in fashion, there is no need to sacrifice form for function, or vice versa. The old rules of fashion have fallen away, giving you the freedom to choose items that work for the occasion and for your tastes. Comfortable clothes allow you to focus on the moment and enjoy the occasion, rather than worrying about, say, a pair of too-tight heels. In the past, if you wore a gown, you were expected to wear high heels. Today, if you wear a gown, you can pair it with a cool pair of sneakers and still walk a red carpet.

ACCESSIBILITY AND COMFORT

It's also important to consider any accessibility needs you may have. For example, if you use a wheelchair, you want clothing that's comfortable for sitting, and easy to get into and out of while sitting. There are many more options of adaptive clothing available today, as we see adaptive-specific brands coming into the market, like Joe & Bella, and existing brands like Tommy Hilfiger and Nike adding adaptive choices. Examples include Velcro closures, full-length zippers, openings to accommodate medical devices, and step-in shoes. I have had clients with arthritis who struggle doing up buttons, so we found pieces with magnetic buttons instead. For a client with a prosthetic arm, we worked with a tailor to customize a few unique pieces for her, adapting sleeves and breakaway snaps. And for anyone with sensory issues, a tag-less shirt can be life changing.

Bringing Together Your Likes and Your Lifestyle

A firm grasp of your Style ID also allows you to apply the science of style and dress seamlessly for any occasion, while being true to your authentic personal style. Say you love the glamour of shimmering fabric and sheer lace, and you go all out wearing pieces like this on the weekends—but on Monday, you feel like you are wearing a costume as you put on a navy suit. You don't feel like your true self. With a clear understanding of the Style Formula, you will be able to discover ways to harness that glam feeling, even for the workplace. You might wear a shimmering top under a navy jacket or find a sharp blazer that has sophisticated lace details. This allows you to show up confident and empowered as you embrace and express your true self every day, not just on the weekends.

Tuning into your personal style sense and putting it into action is a journey—a progression that continues to refine and evolve throughout your life, because your style is a reflection of your authentic self, which changes with each new experience. You will embrace new fashions, try new things, and get bored of others. But once you are in touch with your unique likes and dislikes, you will take note and have a strong thread that connects it all. That underlying connection to your preferences will guide you, helping you to choose the pieces that make you feel good in what you wear and serving as a reliable foundation for your style journey through every phase of life.

Your likes and lifestyle are essential to unfolding your Style ID. Now that you have some sense of how that works, you have everything you need to start building your perfect wardrobe. In the next chapter, you'll start implementing everything you've learned.

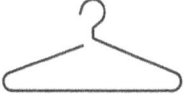

To the Closet: Define Your Likes and Lifestyle

The first exercise here will help you determine your style preferences, so you can start identifying that personal authenticity that makes you feel confident and true to yourself. The second is about analyzing your lifestyle, so you can build a wardrobe to match.

Exercise 1: Analyzing Your Mood Board

Mood boarding is my favorite activity for helping my clients tap into their authentic style. Use the list of resources outlined earlier in this chapter. You can make a physical mood board, or there are plenty of digital tools you can use to create virtual mood boards. The most important thing is to pick a method that works best for you, in a format that compiles everything and that you can refer to whenever you like.

As you're putting together your mood board, go with your first instincts. Again, your style is more than clothing. Your mood board can include everything from hair and makeup looks to interior design and historical figures or favorite TV characters. We are looking to expose you to lots of different ideas and aesthetics so that you will naturally begin to identify favorites. And when you find something you love, follow that thread and see where it goes. It may lead you to even more undiscovered things that you love.

As your mood board grows, you can also delete images that no longer appeal to you. When your mood board starts to feel cohesive, begin looking for patterns. Is there a common thread? Certain colors, cuts, or fabrics? Can you identify a common vibe—say classic but casual, simple but chic? Are there items that appear repeatedly, say blazers and denim, or colors that appear to be favorites, like burgundy, pink, or navy? For nonfashion items, are there similarities you notice? Say, colors or materials that appear repeatedly?

Now, with your mood board in hand, find a piece of clothing that you love and wear all the time, and compare it to your mood board. I bet you will see some similarities. Maybe that favorite piece you're holding is a delicate sundress with a ruffled hem, and your mood board has a lot of delicate, feminine vibes, like pastels and flowers. Or maybe that favorite piece you're holding is a pair of ripped, dark-denim jeans, and your mood board has a lot of distressed pieces and leather jackets.

Now, find a piece of clothing you *never* wear and compare it to your mood board. Chances are, it won't quite fit with your style vision. I often spot these outliers in a client's closet—many times, they're gifts from a well-intentioned husband, friend, or family member. It's simply not something they would have chosen for themselves.

With all this knowledge in hand of what you do and don't like, it will get easier to articulate your personal style. The key is to find patterns on both sides of the equation. Think of it as a process of gathering data points. You can then analyze all that information to figure out exactly who you are and aren't in terms of your authentic style. Now, write down a few words or phrases that capture elements of your personal style you see emerging in these patterns.

Exercise 2: Creating Your Lifestyle Pie Chart

Coming up with a general ratio of how you spend your time can help guide your overall wardrobe composition. If you only go out on the town once or twice a month, you probably don't need a closet full of fancy clubwear. If you go to the gym every morning, you want to make sure you have plenty of workout clothes. Your occupation is a big part of how you spend your days. Are you a college student going to class every morning? Are you a young professional balancing a career and after-work socializing? Are you an executive, presenting to

THE STYLE FORMULA

board members and investors? Are you a stay-at-home parent with young kids that keep you on the go from sunrise to sundown?

The first step to creating your lifestyle pie chart is to create a list of all the activities in your life, from walking the dog to going to the office. Considering an entire month, list out all of those activities and write the number of times you attend each activity in a month next to it. This exercise encourages a realistic view of your lifestyle by focusing on the way you actually spend your time (versus the way you wish you spent your time).

The next step is to look for crossover. Consider your list and create general categories of activities for which you can wear the same thing. Add up the total number of outfits you need in that combined category. For example, if your gym clothes and walk-the-dog outfits are basically the same, put them together under a "Workout Clothes" category. For me, my "Work" category is a high number, since I also wear my work clothes to meet friends during the day or go to meetings at my children's school. I therefore invest in proportionally more of these pieces.

This process leaves you with a very good estimate of the proportional need for each type or category of outfits in straightforward, numerical terms. Now, you can map out the ratio of how you spend your days in a pie chart to create a clear visual representation.

When we get into building a wardrobe and shopping in the next chapter, you can create a second pie chart that estimates what is currently in your wardrobe. By comparing what you currently have in your closet to the needs summarized in your pie chart, you can see what activity areas are underrepresented and what activity areas are

CHAPTER 6

overrepresented. For example, maybe you have loads of great heels but not a lot of comfortable shoes, despite having a very active, on-your-feet lifestyle. This information will help you as you review your wardrobe and create a targeted shopping list to fill in the gaps.

Unlock more style insights! Scan the QR code for exclusive content and interactive exercises to deepen your understanding of the chapter's key concepts and help you further explore your Style ID.

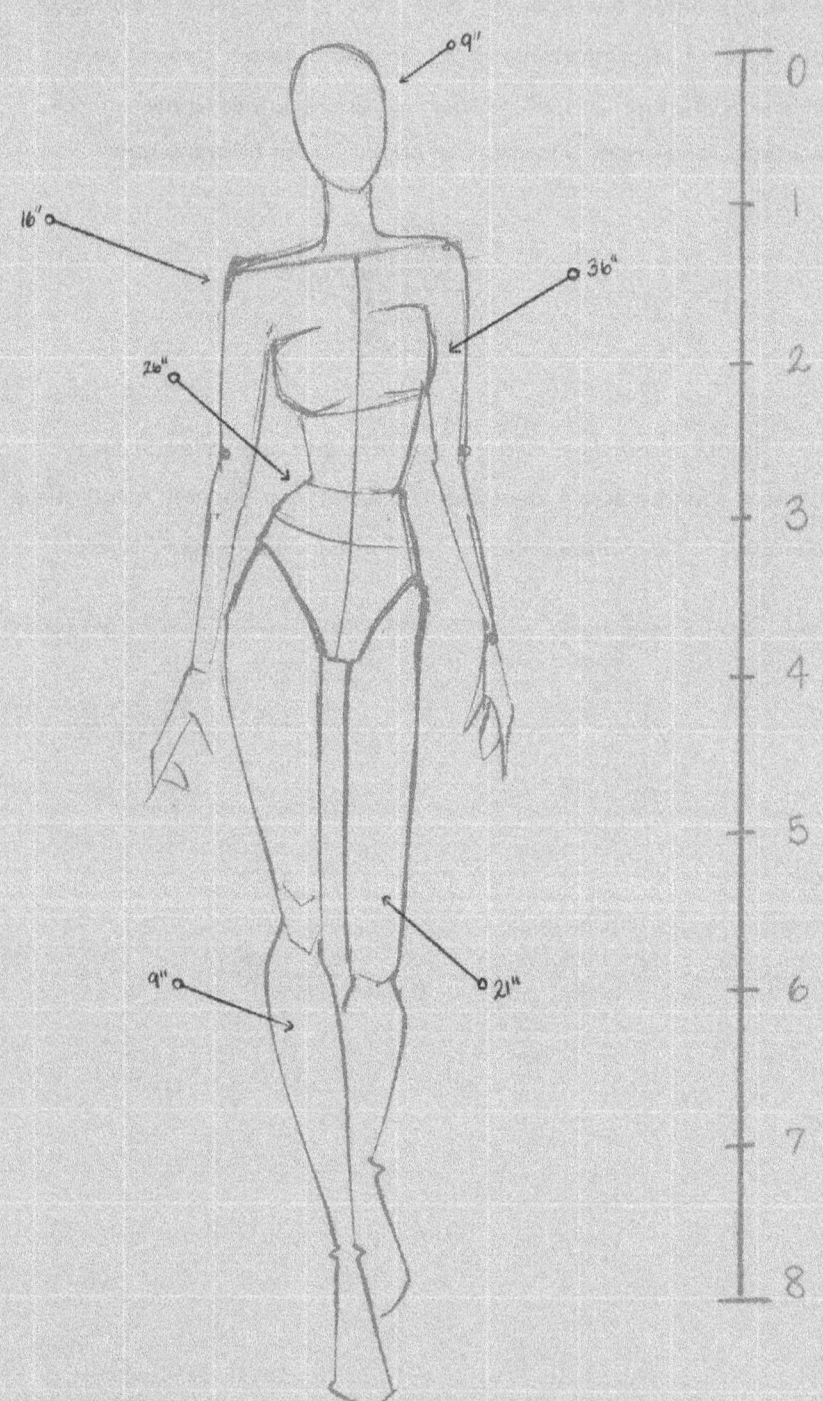

PART III
Crafting Your Closet

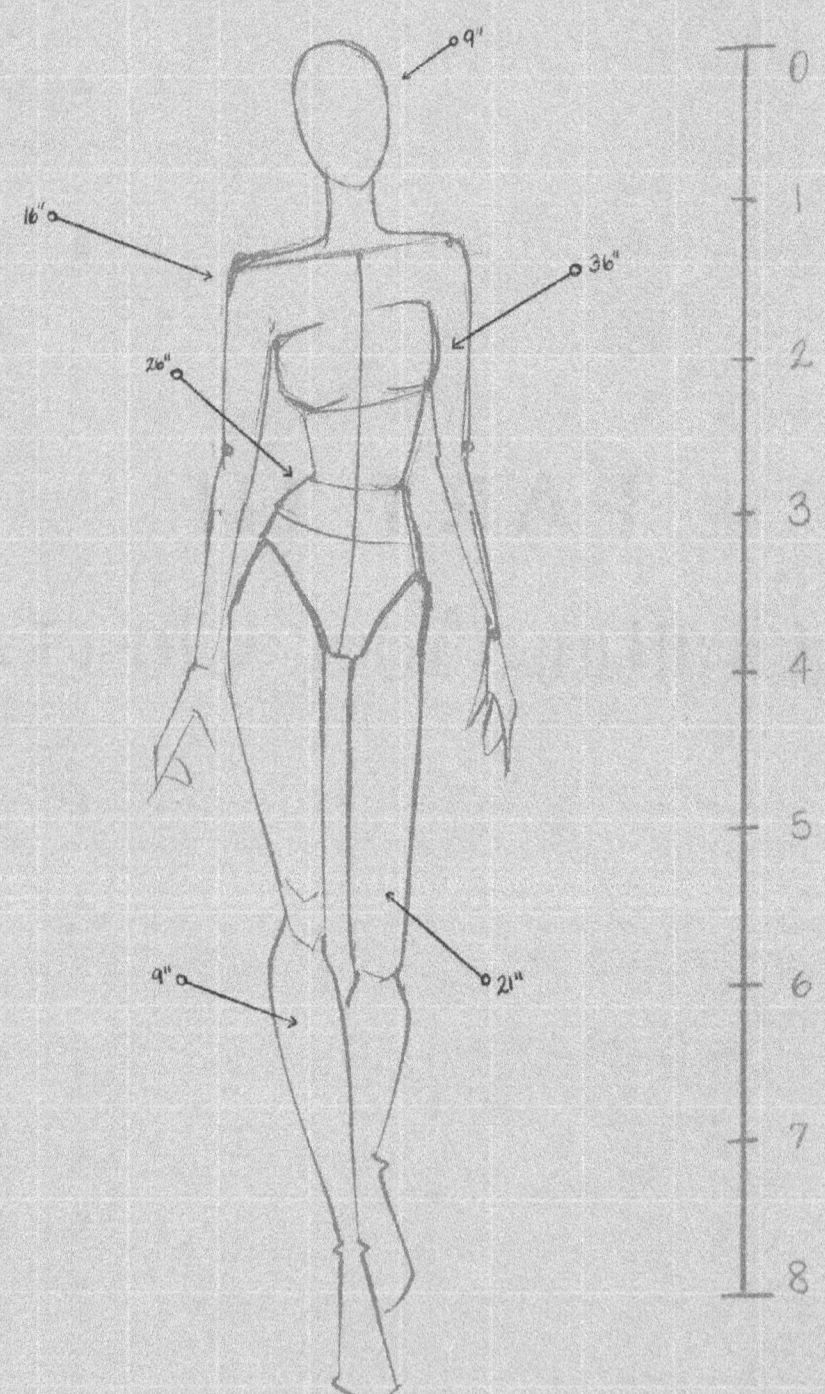

CHAPTER 7

Building Your Foundational Wardrobe

As you come to understand your Style ID, you will be pleasantly surprised at how easy it is to navigate your closet with confidence. It's an exciting moment. By the time we step into the closet, I often see that glimmer in a client's eye—the joy of "getting it" as they view what they already own through a fresh lens. This is where the fun really begins—building a wardrobe and curating outfits you feel great in and want to wear, again and again. In these final two chapters, you'll learn how to select pieces that work for you, aligning with your style goals and turning each piece into an asset, as well as how to style them in a way that reflects your preferences and lifestyle.

One client I worked with—I will call her Jacqueline—wanted to start her closet edit by tackling her leggings and skinny jeans. This was back when both were popular, and leggings were even gracing red carpets. Jacqueline had stocked up on the trend and had plenty of skinny jeans and leggings to choose from. However, she was self-conscious about how these bottoms accentuated her lower half, so she always paired them with long, flowing tops to cover herself.

She had lots of different colors and patterns across these items, so the outfits still had some variety. She would pair dark-gray skinny denim with a blue drapey sweater one day, and black leggings with a flowing purple blouse the next. There was an illusion of difference. But the combinations were essentially all the same, with each piece doing the same job.

Instead of having a variety of cuts or styles, her bottoms were all skinny cut and very fitted, while the blouses were all cut long enough to cover and flow over her bottom. This combination of preferences resulted in limited clothing selections and led to repetitive outfits. As a result, her wardrobe was not balanced or fully aligned with her preferences.

This combination of top and bottom also impacted her footwear and accessories. In fall and winter, she always paired her skinny jeans and leggings with knee-high boots. If she tried to wear ankle boots, there was a gap between her shoe and the bottom of her pants she didn't like. Similarly, she did not like to carry small bags or purses, because they got lost in her blousy tops. She would reach for a large, oversized handbag as a result, even when she would have liked to carry something lighter and less bulky, like a clutch.

Jacqueline found her wardrobe limiting, which is why she came to me. She was seeking versatility. My mission was to give Jacqueline more options in her closet, building her wardrobe based on her Style ID. And that is what I want to do for you too.

Wardrobe building is the next step in the Style Formula, and everything you've learned so far is designed to guide you. With the foundation in place, the real fun begins as you craft a wardrobe that truly works for you!

It begins with a foundational understanding of the composition of the wardrobe before diving into closet edits or shopping for new items. By first uncovering what you truly need, you can make more intentional decisions about what to keep, let go of, or add. What does a well-rounded wardrobe look like? In this chapter, we create a blueprint to guide you, examining closet composition and how it relates to your own needs and preferences. We'll discuss details like balance, functionality, and budget to help you create your perfect wardrobe.

The Three Categories of Clothes in Your Wardrobe

In its simplest form, your wardrobe is made up of three categories of items. First, there are what we at Unfoldid call your ID Essentials, which are your basics, the foundational pieces that anchor your wardrobe. Then, there are Signature Pieces, which are those key pieces that speak to your authentic personal style yet are still versatile enough to wear in many different ways. Finally, there are the Statement Pieces, which provide variety and interest to your outfits.

At Unfoldid, the first step in our closet edit is to check through and refine these categories, seeing which pieces the client already has in the closet, and which are missing and need to go on the shopping list. Differentiating clothing into these groups helps to create easy reference points for you as you build, edit, and maintain your wardrobe.

This approach will also help with building a targeted shopping list, keeping you on track and avoiding a more haphazard approach. In the same way that going to the grocery store without a list or shopping while we are hungry can lead to a fuller grocery cart, when we shop for clothes without parameters, it's easy to end up with too much of what we don't need and miss those essential pieces that will fill out our wardrobe. With the right guardrails, we can pick up missing must-have items and avoid duplicates, expanding the wardrobe efficiently and effectively.

The formula to a successful shopping list is to be as detailed as possible. For example, instead of just "navy dress," consider details like fabric, cut, color, and texture. You might want a navy dress in lightweight cotton that cinches at the waist and has a V-neck. This is where you're putting into practice all you have learned about your Style ID. The more detailed your description, the better and the easier it will be to find a piece you love. Plus, with many retailers now offering advanced online filters, you can fine-tune your search to match these exact parameters, making shopping both more efficient and intentional.

It is also helpful to note on your shopping list if you have an overabundance in any of these three categories of clothing. This can help guide current and future shopping. For example, I have seen closets full of great ID Essentials in perfect neutrals but hardly any Signature or Statement Pieces to add variety and reflect personal style. I have also seen closets bursting with fantastic and fun Statement Pieces—but due to a lack of ID Essentials, it was difficult to create complete outfits.

Let's look in more detail at each of these wardrobe categories:

ID ESSENTIALS

These are the items you wear the most frequently—your top ten. They are the foundation of a functioning wardrobe, supporting and balancing out the rest of your wardrobe and ensuring that you always have the right pieces to complete any outfit. These are also your investment pieces. Since you wear them often and keep them longer, this is where you can confidently spend more money on high-quality, timeless options. And because of their frequent rotation, even a higher price tag results in an excellent cost-per-wear (CPW)—something we will look at more closely later in the chapter.

SIGNATURE PIECES

Signature Pieces are those key pieces that anchor your personal style but are still versatile enough to be worn in many different ways. These pieces should not be overly bold but solidly reflect what you love. They tend to strike the balance between not too dressy or too casual, according to your style. While an ID Essentials shoe may be black, a Signature pair may be red or gold, assuming those colors speak to your authentic style. Any item, from layers to bags, pants, or tops, can be a Signature Piece, as long as it fully reflects your style and has versatility. Like ID Essentials, Signature Pieces should be well constructed, a great fit, and ideally seasonless. Likewise, because Signature Pieces are worn often and have a big impact on your look, you will want to spend more on them relative to their versatility and timelessness.

STATEMENT PIECES

Statement Pieces give your outfits interest and variety. They highlight different sides of your style and can be paired with most anything in your closet. Wear them mixed together for a bold look, with Signature Pieces for a toned-down version, or with your basics to give them a lift. These pieces are what create your high-low mix—less expensive pieces will look elevated when you pair them with ID Essentials and Signature Pieces. These don't need to be as versatile, but they should still follow the rule of four, meaning they work with at least four items in your closet. These pieces don't need to last more than a couple of seasons, so there is no need to spend a lot here. Find pieces that fit your Style ID and look great but don't overspend.

Six Criteria for Your ID Essentials (and Beyond)

Now, let's take a step back and explore some key criteria to guide you in selecting pieces that will build a versatile, lasting wardrobe. These six criteria serve as a guide for choosing the most efficient and adaptable pieces, helping you spend smart and create a collection that stands the test of time. The more criteria a piece meets, the more value and versatility it brings to your wardrobe. Since your ID Essentials are the most efficient and versatile pieces in your wardrobe, they should align with all six criteria outlined below.

The goal is to be mindful of these criteria as you spend your clothing budget, using them as a framework to make intentional purchases. While Statement or Signature Pieces don't need to meet all six, understanding these guidelines can help you maximize your wardrobe's versatility and value. This approach also leaves room in your budget for unique, less-efficient pieces that simply bring you joy.

You will use these criteria when editing your wardrobe and when shopping, so it's good to keep them at hand. Here is an overview of the six key criteria:

- **Seasonless:** Look for a seasonless fabric and cut that can be worn year round, making the most of your clothing dollars. For example, linen is a wonderful staple in summer. But it is not seasonless, as it works best during hotter months. In contrast, a medium-weight, stretch wool jacket can be worn on a cool summer night or in the middle of a New England winter.

- **Neutral:** Choose one neutral hue from your color palette. If you already have some ID Essentials in a great neutral from your palette, I recommend continuing to build that one color, creating a full set of ID Essentials. If you want a more extensive wardrobe, you can later add a second set of ID Essentials in another color. This is the most efficient way to build your wardrobe over time.

- **Great fit and cut:** The item should have a cut that aligns with your body architecture and have great fit. When you slip it on, it should not pull or gap or restrict your movement. It should fit or be tailored just right.

- **Simple:** Seek out pieces that are clean and trendproof, so they can transform into anything you need. They should reflect your authentic style but be versatile, so it's best to avoid features like sequins. For example, ripped denim is more difficult to dress up, while clean denim can be easily dressed up or down with a distressed tee or a blazer for work.

- **Style:** Make sure the look is authentic to you. Look for styles you love that fit your lifestyle and authentic personal style. If you have a softer or more delicate style, you might look for a flowing skirt or maybe one with lace detail, for example.

- **Quality:** Quality pieces that allow for multiple wears and last for years will help stretch your clothing dollars. Look at details like materials, stitching, and quality of hardware (zippers, buckles, buttons) to assess quality.

ID Essentials: The List

As I mentioned, the ID Essentials are ten core items that I recommend everyone keep in their closet. Exactly what these items look like will depend on your Style ID and therefore take into account all the components of the Style Formula. We already talked about everybody's LBD looks different. If black is not in your color palette, your LBD might be charcoal gray or navy, for instance. And the cut of an LBD will vary in line with your architecture. At the same time, your lifestyle could determine characteristics such as material and hardware, like zippers versus buttons. Finally, what you like in an LBD is going to be unique from what anyone else likes in an LBD.

This version of the ID Essentials list is designed for those with a more feminine aesthetic. A version styled with a more masculine aesthetic is also available on the Unfoldid website. This list aims to cover the broadest selection of pieces you might need—but it can be adapted to specific preferences. For example, if you prefer a more gender-neutral look, you can skip the skirt and instead opt for a pair of dress pants that fill the same role. In this case, it could be a pant that is a step dressier than a work pant. Or a dress can be replaced with a pantsuit or a coordinated top and bottom.

At Unfoldid, I also developed a list of ID Essential Shoes and ID Essential Accessories for our team to use with clients. The shoe list is a good example of how essentials prioritize versatility. If you have a good nude dress shoe—nude meaning it matches your skin tone—then you have a pair of dress shoes to wear with any dress, skirt, or pair of shorts you own. If you have a pair of gorgeous red pumps, on the other hand, you lose that versatility.

For now, I want to focus on the ten essentials for clothes and explain *why* I consider them essential. Remember, each of these pieces must meet all six criteria discussed in the previous section to qualify as an ID Essential. Since these pieces are your workhorses that anchor your wardrobe, you will invest more in them and want them to hit all six points. It may take a bit more time to find that just-right piece, but it will be so worth it when you reach for that staple again and again all throughout the year.

LITTLE BLACK DRESS

This simple, clean look is as versatile as it gets. It can be a last-minute lifesaver for events, meetings, nights out, funerals, and even a coffee date.

What to look for: Pick a quality fabric in a dark neutral that fits your color palette. I recommend an LBD with short sleeves that you can wear solo when it's warm out or add layers over for cooler weather.

Ways to wear it: Add a sparkling necklace, blazer, or sweater to change the look of your LBD. Pair it with any footwear, from flats to heels.

PANTS YOU LOVE

Pants are a step up from denim but still more casual and wearable than a skirt. They can be worn to work, for shopping, and beyond.

What to look for: Straight or wider leg cuts tend to flatter every body architecture. Pick a quality fabric that drapes. Depending on the length, have them hemmed to a midpoint, so that they're flexible to wear with all your shoes.

Ways to wear it: Pants can pair with everything from graphic tees and sneakers to a flowy blouse with heels.

JACKET, BLAZER, OR CARDIGAN

Whichever of these three you choose, according to your needs and style, it should give you a clean, versatile layer to work into many different outfits. You could also start with one and add the other two later.

What to look for: Opt for a seasonless fabric in a dark neutral. Make sure the fit and length suit your body architecture. Many lifestyles benefit from both a soft version (like a cardigan) as well as a more tailored version (like a fitted blazer).

Ways to wear it: This is a super versatile piece you can pair with anything from suit bottoms to ripped jeans. Depending on the season and occasion, it can serve as outerwear, be thrown on over a T-shirt for a video call, or be worn in the boardroom.

JEANS

This one is pretty self-explanatory, since jeans are a wardrobe staple for almost everybody. It's the go-to that you can wear to the park, to coffee, to dinner … wherever your busy day takes you. And it is the perfect piece to instantly dress down a look.

What to look for: To maintain versatility prioritize styles that range from straight-leg to bootcut or tailored wide-leg cuts, which work with your body architecture. Pick a dark, clean wash that will be nice enough for dressier looks but basic enough to be worn as daily denim.

Ways to wear it: Denim can be a nice go-to for long days when you want to look put together but keep it comfortable. You can easily transition jeans for different occasions, depending on what you pair them with: a blazer with a blouse and loafers for work, sneakers and a T-shirt for errands, or sequins and heels for a night out.

KNEE-LENGTH SKIRT

This piece is perfect for when a dress feels too formal, but pants won't work (or you just aren't in the mood for them—say, because it's ninety degrees Fahrenheit outside).

What to look for: Choose a knee-length skirt in a great, understated cut. Clean, neutral colors are good for both work and play.

Ways to wear it: A knee-length skirt can be worn with your favorite top for a baby shower or brunch, or adapted for work when paired with a blazer. It can also be dressed down with a graphic tee and flats for a casual lunch.

CLASSIC "WHITE" LONG-SLEEVE SHIRT

With more coverage than a T-shirt, this wardrobe staple can be worn solo or layered. The "white" will depend on your color palette.

What to look for: Choose between a classic button-down, flowy blouse, or simple crew in a white or creamy-colored fabric.

Ways to wear it: Wear tucked or untucked, under a jacket or sweater, or layered with a scarf or necklace. Sticking with white makes it easy to pair with any of your bottoms and complete any outfit combination.

"WHITE" LIGHT AND DARK SHORT-SLEEVE T-SHIRT

This is a go-to in warmer weather that can be layered but is also dressy enough to be worn alone. Have one light-colored T-shirt and one dark-colored T-shirt (they can even be the same cut, brand, and style if you find something you love).

What to look for: This item should be substantial enough to wear on its own. Look for quality material that won't wrinkle or wear easily. Sticking with a white and dark neutral from your palette makes it easy to pair with any of your bottoms and complete any outfit.

Ways to wear it: A quality T-shirt can pair with pretty much any bottom, be it jeans, a skirt, or pants. Dress it up with accessories like a statement necklace or keep it simple and accessory-free. Layer it under jackets, blazers, or cardigans to complete your look.

THIN KNIT

Consider this your T-shirt for the colder months. It's easy to layer with all year round.

What to look for: You will want a suitably thin knit, so you can layer it under jackets, bulky cardigans, and other toppers. Choose solid colors and stick with thin fabrics like cashmere, merino wool, or synthetic.

Ways to wear it: Wear it over a T-shirt or tank top on a cool summer evening, or under a jacket or blazer for cold winter days to give yourself an easy and comfortable extra layer to keep warm.

THE "ANY OCCASION" TOP

Stylish and practical, the "any occasion" top is designed to fit your lifestyle. One person's "any occasion" will vary from another's. This is the simplest way to switch up your look and create multiple outfit combinations with your existing pieces by adding a pop of color or print.

What to look for: Look for a color or print in a versatile hue from your color palette.

Ways to wear it: The name speaks for itself—this one is for any occasion. Pair it with jeans for brunch or a skirt for the office. It's an easy way to add interest and create outfits.

A LOUNGE PANT

Skip the pajama bottoms and still look put together when you invest in these. Lounge pants are great for travel and lazy days with friends and family.

What to look for: Look for a sophisticated option in a flattering cut with lots of stretch.

Ways to wear it: Depending on the season, a lounge pant can be paired with your thin knit or T-shirt/shell, and then leveled up or down with accessories.

Imagine that you have been building up your wardrobe and now have all your ID Essentials and they are amazing. Over time, you will need to slowly replace these pieces—but because they are higher quality, they will last longer. Each season, you can put aside a portion of your clothing budget to revamp ID Essentials, typically around 25 percent. Each year, you might also add to or refine your Signature Pieces with a portion of your budget—maybe another 25 percent. This leaves 50 percent of your budget, which you can spend on either fun, less expensive Statement Pieces that are meant to be replaced and turned more often, or on a higher-quality splurge piece that will last.

Once you have a clear understanding of how wardrobes are built, it can help you to spend smart, have pieces you need and love, and create more outfits. This strategy should not prevent you from buying something your heart wants. Instead, my goal is to help you maximize your clothing budget so you can splurge on an item you love or justify a purchase that you know will make getting dressed easier.

For example, last year, two of my favorite thin-knit sweaters finally fell apart. I knew they were ID Essentials, so as winter sales rolled through, I picked up replacements, getting great, high-quality pieces at bargain prices. This year, my neutral-brown blazer needs replacing, and I need to update a few of my basic tees, but everything else is in good shape. So, since I have some leftover in my budget, I will likely pick up a pair of hot-pink sneakers I've been eyeing.

Closet Editing: Assessing What You Already Own

Odds are that you already have some great pieces in your closet. Once you have your Style ID, you can easily take inventory of your current wardrobe. We have already defined the structure and elements of a balanced wardrobe. Closet editing can help you see where you stand and determine what's missing. This is the process of cross-checking what you already own against your Style ID, and also against the key categories of ID Essentials, Signature Pieces, and Statement Pieces. This method ensures that the items you own will work for you effortlessly and creates space for any additional pieces to expand your outfit options.

When you take inventory of your closet, I always recommend trying on any piece that you are not sure about. This is the best way to determine how details like fit and cut align with your Style ID. You will want to set aside plenty of time for this process, so you don't feel rushed—taking your time with this process can make a big difference. By going through your entire wardrobe with an eye toward your Style ID, it allows you to thoughtfully let go of pieces that don't fit your preferences and no longer reflect who you are. This kind of decluttering creates the space you need to transform your closet into the wardrobe you want, where each piece feels purposeful and works for you.

To get started, focus first on the items on the ID Essentials list. For example, you might start by pulling out all your black or neutral pants and seeing if any qualifies as an ID Essential. If not, add the item to your shopping list. For all the other black or neutral pants, use Unfoldid's Closet Edit Flowchart to help you decide if they stay or go.

At Unfoldid, we use this flowchart to guide the closet-editing process and support intentional wardrobe choices. I've highlighted the most salient points here, but you can find the full flowchart later in this chapter. As you go through your closet item by item—including those boxes stored in the attic—ask yourself these questions for each piece you try on:

- Is it in good shape? Does the item have obvious signs of wear and tear, or is it damaged? If there is damage, can it be salvaged? For example, a broken zipper can be replaced.

- Is it current with your lifestyle? As we evolve, so do the clothes we wear. Now that remote work has become normalized, many offices have become more casual, and many people no longer need their old office wear, for instance.

- Does it fit your preferences? Is the piece in line with your body architecture, palette, likes, and lifestyle?

- Does it fit you? If not, is it possible to tailor it to fit? If shirt sleeves or pant legs are too long, it's easy enough to get them hemmed, for example, while other alterations may be too difficult or expensive.

- Have you worn it in the past one to two years? If not, how many of the boxes above does it check? The reason you haven't worn it may be that it doesn't fit your Style ID or it's damaged, for example. Or it may be that you didn't have that meeting or event last year. Determine if the reason is something you can fix or if it's time to let it go.

- Do you have at least four other pieces that it works with to create outfits?

- Is it a duplicate or triplicate? Do you have others that are almost identical? Or several others that are similar and do the same job in your wardrobe?

My goal is to have everything in your wardrobe meet these criteria. That said, wardrobe building is a process. As you go through your closet, if you feel like too many items in a category are not quite right, simply pare down. But hold onto those almost-right pieces while you are looking for that perfect piece to replace them with.

CHAPTER 7

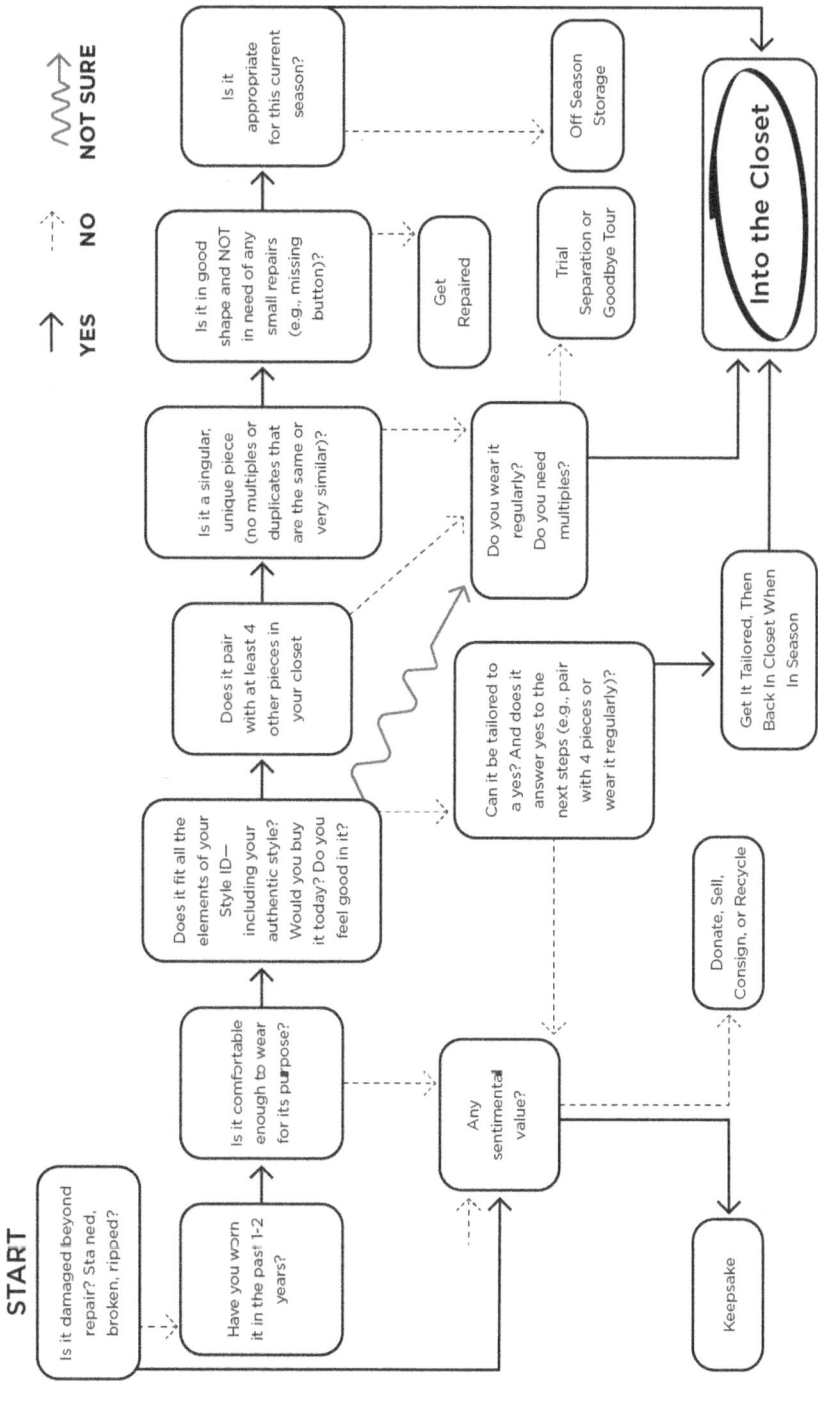

An actionable closet edit flowchart

So, what *does* happen to the things that you decide to edit out of your wardrobe? You have a few options.

- If something is really destroyed, it does need to be discarded—ideally, try to send it to an environmentally friendly textiles recycling program.
- Items that are still in good condition but don't work for you can be donated.
- If you have higher-tier items that are in good shape, you might consider consigning them or selling them online.
- Sentimental items can be repurposed. That college tee can be kept around to stuff handbags, for example, while parts of your wedding dress can be used to create something new. Say, take the lace trim and use it to make a throw pillow cover.

What happens if you have an item you are not sure about? As you can see in the flowchart, in cases like these, I like to suggest what a stylist on my team, Amanda Sanford-Smith, has termed the "goodbye tour." Let's say you have a top you haven't worn in years, but you can't quite bring yourself to part with it. Wear it for a full day and see how it makes you feel.

I use this method often and am always amazed at what I uncover: "Ah, now I remember, these pants pinch at that one spot on the side," or "This top is scratchy at the neck." Or, in some cases, it might be, "This is great! Why do I never wear this?" However, from my experience, the more likely possibility is that you will quickly discover why you never reach for the item. Maybe there is something off about the fit, or the fabric is uncomfortable. Whatever the issue is, you can then confidently edit that item out of your closet knowing that you gave it one last fair chance.

If there are items you are bored of but still inherently like, you can simply rest them for a season. A fabulous sweater that you wore twice a week last winter may not feel exciting this winter, but after taking a season off, you will be happy to see it again. Timeless pieces, like trench coats, never go out of style and often cycle back into trends—making them ideal candidates for a seasonal rest.

Finally, if there is something that you still are on the fence about, you can do a trial separation. Get a box and put all the "not sure" items in it and put it away in the attic or in the back of your closet. Then, see if you miss anything and feel a need to take it back out. If after a year you have never thought about the items in the box, you know you can let them go without even opening it. Just like the rest of this journey, closet editing is a process that you repeat and revisit as you evolve.

Once your closet is decluttered, it's the perfect time to revisit the lifestyle pie charts we discussed in the previous chapter. With a clearer view, you'll find it much easier to assess how much of each category is represented in your closet. Estimating the percentage of clothing in each of your categories and then comparing it to your lifestyle pie chart can reveal any imbalances. This is valuable information that can be helpful to note on your shopping list.

This is also a good time to consider making a mini palette composed of a few colors chosen from your personal palette. While every color in your personal palette works together, a mini palette can focus your wardrobe, especially during the beginning phase. It provides a tighter guide that can be expanded over time. A good mini palette consists of neutrals, leading colors, and accent colors, all from your seasonal palette. The two neutrals should include a light and a dark; you can pick the neutrals that most speak to you or, for efficiency's sake, pick the two neutrals that are most dominant in your closet postedit (assuming they still resonate with your personal style).

Some people find it easier to pick neutrals after picking leading and accent colors first. Pick three leading colors that anchor your personal style—colors that you instinctively love and that work well together and with your neutrals. Check your mood board or your closet for inspiration. Then pick four accent colors that resonate with you and work well with your leading colors and neutrals in your mini palette. A mini palette is great for focusing a disparate wardrobe or building a fresh wardrobe, guiding your choices of ID Essentials, Signature Pieces, and Statement Pieces.

Shopping with Intention

At this stage, you've explored the foundations for your shopping list. You've learned how to identify the key items missing from your ID Essentials, Signature Pieces, and Statement Pieces. You've gained an understanding of how to conduct a closet edit to assess what you already have and what might be lacking. You've also created a lifestyle pie chart and mood board, giving you strong guidelines to inform your future choices. Altogether, you now have the tools to confidently identify what you're looking for. This understanding can make the process even more enjoyable and rewarding, allowing you to be selective and patient as you search for those perfect additions.

When you shop, these questions can help guide you further:

- Does it stand on its own as a great piece that fits my Style ID?
- Is it a perfect fit, or can it be efficiently tailored?
- Is it the right quality level that I want for this piece?

- Do I need it? Is it on my shopping list? If not, do I already own something like it that does the same job or fulfils the same role in my wardrobe?

- Does it fit my lifestyle needs and activities, and round out my wardrobe balance?

- Does it work with the rule of four and go with at least four other items in my wardrobe?

- Does the piece fit my budget right now? And is it the best use of my budget?

If the answers to the above questions are no, but you still love the item, that does not mean you should not purchase it. Even though it may not pass the questions above, asking these questions will allow you to make a conscious choice to splurge on an item, and you will be aware of your decision and the elements this piece is missing. It makes the purchase a conscious choice, not an impulse buy.

Budget is a definite consideration when shopping. In order to get the most out of your shopping dollars, I always suggest spending the most on your ID Essentials. Those are the pieces you are going to wear the most frequently, and they will anchor and elevate anything you pair with them—think high-low dressing, where an inexpensive sequin tank looks special and expensive under a beautiful well-tailored blazer. You will get a better CPW by spending more on the blazer you wear fifty days of the year than you will by spending more on the sequin tank you wear once per year.

CPW is a metric that will help you understand the real price and value of your clothes based on how many times you wear them. To calculate the CPW of an item, simply divide its price tag by the number of times you've worn it or plan to wear it. For example, if you spent $30 on a sweater and so far have worn it 10 times, its current CPW is $3 per wear. If you purchase a pair of high-quality designer jeans for $250, but you plan to wear them twice a week all year round (52 weeks × 2 = 104), your CPW for the year is $2.40. As you can see, the jeans cost much more up front but actually have a lower CPW after only one year—and a quality jean could last two, three, or even five or more years.

CPW is also helpful in understanding the costs of fast fashion, which tends to be cheaper but has a higher CPW. I often see closets full of twelve to fifteen pairs of black pants that are nearly identical. But as we go through them, it becomes clear most have some issue preventing them from being just right. The money we spend on ten pairs that are not quite right could be spent on one fantastic pair that we reach for again and again, saving time and energy when getting dressed. It can be hard to spend a big piece of our budget all at once on one expensive pair of black pants, perfect as they may be. But when we step back and consider the real cost of purchasing ten pairs of less-expensive, less-than-perfect pants, it is clear that the one great pair of black pants will likely cost us less in the long run—and will look amazing every time we wear them because of their quality.

CHAPTER 7

> ### Calculating cost-per-wear of a sweater
>
> Fast fashion sweater with a lifespan of 20 wears
> Original sale price: $30
> Number of times worn: 20
> Cost per wear: 30 ÷ 20 = $1.50 per wear
>
> High-quality sweater with a lifespan of 100 wears
> Original sale price: $80
> Number of times worn: 100
> Cost per wear: 80 ÷ 100 = $.80 per wear

An example of how CPW calculations might work

I recognize that everyone has different budgets and abilities to invest in high-quality or sustainable pieces, and this calculation can be helpful as you shop. We all want to allocate our clothing dollars in a way that best serves our needs. There's often an assumption that shopping means buying a whole new wardrobe, but as I've mentioned, this process takes time—so you don't need to make big purchases right away. Plus, as you build a more cohesive wardrobe, you will find that your spending becomes much more efficient. Each new piece will expand your outfit options, and you won't need to keep buying additional items just to make outfits work, because everything will mix and match seamlessly. Additionally, investing in quality, timeless pieces means replacing items less often.

Common Shopping Habits to Be Aware Of

When you start shopping, it's also helpful to be aware of common habits that people tend to fall into. Last-minute shopping can result in shopping in a hurry, for example. When you're in a rush, you may end up grabbing something that works for right now but not take the time to consider whether it works with the rest of your wardrobe, your Style ID, or your budget.

Approach shopping knowing it will take time to find that perfect piece, but it will be so worth it when you do. Whether you are shopping in person or online, use the tools we've developed, like your targeted shopping list to help keep you focused. For online shopping, many websites have filters that match nicely with elements of your Style ID, allowing you to sort based on necklines, sleeve styles, colors, and more.

Pursuing sales, deals, and discounts can help you build your wardrobe more economically if you are making intentional purchases, but this can also lead to overbuying. I will be the first to admit, I love a sale. However, research has shown that people who are presented with a discounted item tend to minimize the financial risk of purchasing it and tend to act more impulsively.[14] While sales can be a great way to get high-quality pieces on a budget, it's also important to be conscious of whether you are purchasing an item because it actually fits your Style ID—or simply because it's a great deal.

---

14 Fernando De Oliviera Santini, Claudio Sampaio, and Marcelo Gattermann Perin, "An Analysis of the Influence of Discount Sales Promotion in Consumer Buying Intent and the Moderating Effects of Attractiveness," *Revista de Administração* 50, no. 4 (December 2015): 416-31.

Finally, don't place too much importance on an item's listed size. When shopping for clothing, what matters most is the fit and cut. Since different brands use different size standards, the listed size of a garment is, to a degree, irrelevant. You might be a medium in one brand and an extra-large in another—knowing this ahead of time helps you look past the label and focus on finding pieces that truly align with your Style ID. This is why it is important to take the time to try things on. There can also be a psychological factor at play; for example, someone might buy a medium, even if a large fits them better. The tendency to say we *are* our size also echoes the external pressures we explored in chapter 2.

The reality is that size labels don't mean much. Brands even engage in "vanity sizing," a tactic designed to flatter consumers and encourage spending. The idea is that if a consumer sees a smaller size works for them, they think about themselves more positively and may be more inclined to buy the product associated with that feeling.[15]

The best way to avoid slipping into any of these shopping habits is to come back to your list and your Style ID. Both keep you focused, helping you spend clothing dollars on what you need and invest in what suits you and makes you feel your best.

From Wardrobe Building to Outfit Building

Once you take the time to build a wardrobe you love, it will be a lot easier to build outfits you love. But that raises the question: How do you create those outfits? How do you know which pants to pair with which top, and how to choose accessories that express your authentic self?

---

15   Alina Shaheen, "Why You Are a Different Size in Different Fashion Brand Store?" *Fashion & Law Journal*, December 2022, https://fashionlawjournal.com/why-you-are-a-different-size-in-different-fashion-brand-store/.

As with everything else we have covered, there are formulas and methods to guide you. Yes, there is art in styling, but it's also grounded in objective science. Using these methods gives you more freedom to enjoy your creative side. You don't have to be blessed with extreme creativity or an artist's eye to create outfits you love. By following a few simple steps and formulas, the process becomes fast, easy, and enjoyable. And that's been our goal all along: to make getting dressed fun. The final chapter walks you through it.

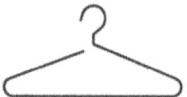

To the Closet: Practice Analyzing Your Wardrobe

Building your perfect wardrobe is about more than seeing like a stylist. There are practical components to think about as well, like purpose and price. These exercises touch on some practicalities we discussed in this chapter and make it easier to analyze your wardrobe—and see how the Style Formula can help you build it.

Exercise 1: Assessing an ID Essential

We talked about the difference between ID Essentials, Signature Pieces, and Statement Pieces, as well as the criteria to apply when buying those pieces—especially the ID Essentials. Pick one item from the ID Essentials list—say, black pants or white long-sleeve shirts—and pull out all the similar items in your closet that could potentially match it. Now, evaluate each piece against the criteria listed in this chapter:

seasonless, neutral, great fit and cut, simple, style, and quality.

How many of the points does each item match? Do any options meet all six criteria? Are there other items from the ID Essentials list in your closet that meet all six? What about non-ID Essentials that check all six boxes? Overall, do you find that most of your closet items meet these criteria—or none at all? Practice objectively evaluating how your clothes fit these criteria and uncover the versatility of the pieces in your closet.

Exercise 2: Run a CPW Analysis

Another exercise that can help you gain a better understanding of your wardrobe is to run a CPW analysis. Start with one of your favorite items in your wardrobe. How many times do you estimate you've worn it? What did it cost you? Now, estimate the CPW, taking the price and dividing it by times worn.

Now try the same for a least favorite item in your wardrobe. Does it have a higher CPW than your favorite? Chances are it does. This exercise can help you gain appreciation for how knowing your Style ID can help you make the most of your clothing dollars.

Unlock more style insights! Scan the QR code for exclusive content and interactive exercises to deepen your understanding of the chapter's key concepts and help you further explore your Style ID.

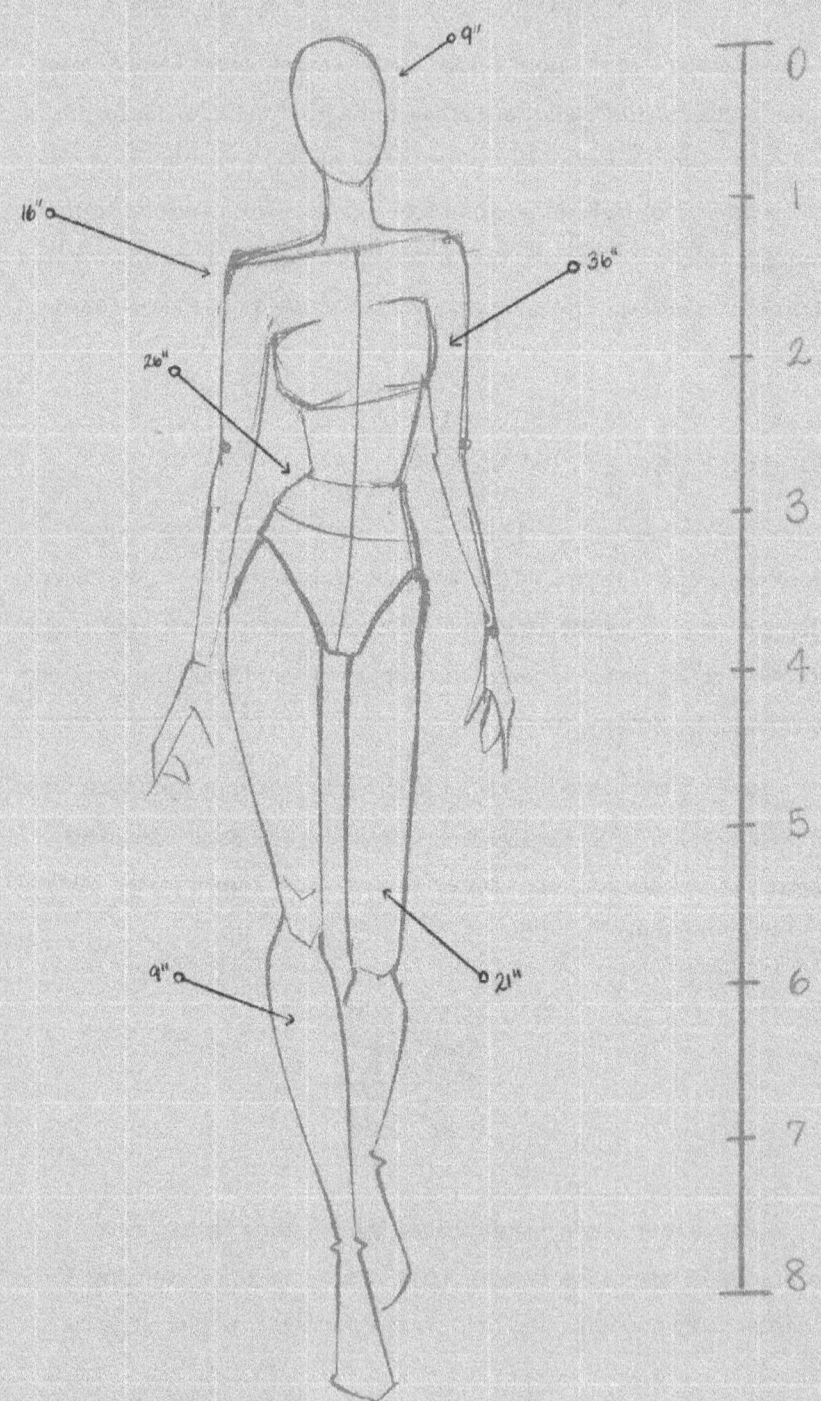

CHAPTER 8

How to Build Easy and Creative Outfits

Now for the fun part: turning everything you've learned about the Style Formula into a creative expression of you. With a wardrobe that works in sync with your silhouette, preferences, and lifestyle, the possibilities open up—whether you're dressing for a casual stroll or a black-tie gala, you'll be amazed at how effortlessly your look comes together.

Take "Tracy," for example. She came to me with a style dilemma that many of us have faced: a multiday wedding event that included everything from cocktail parties to an elegant rehearsal dinner. Tracy had several pieces she liked, but she was stuck, unsure of how to create enough distinct looks without running out to buy something new. And she didn't just want to fit in; she wanted to look amazing on the day itself and in photos that would last a lifetime.

As we sifted through her closet, I pulled out a dark shift dress—a classic, understated piece that skimmed her frame beautifully, straight down from the shoulder and cinching at the waist. The cut and color were a perfect match for her palette and architecture, but Tracy looked at it skeptically. "Isn't this kind of boring?" she asked, worried that it would look too safe or even stale for such an occasion.

This was the kind of challenge I love—helping my client see the potential in a piece they already own. Tracy's style was sleek, modern, and a little edgy, so I suggested pairing the shift dress with a fitted black sweater for added texture and a cool, modern twist. We swapped her plain shoes for sleek burgundy heels and layered on statement accessories—a bold necklace and a chunky ring that added just the right amount of drama.

The transformation was instant. She stood in front of the mirror and smiled. "Wow, I look so cool!" In that moment, she saw the shift dress in a new light—not as "boring" but as the perfect canvas for her personal style. And the best part? She didn't have to buy a single new piece. Everything she needed was already in her closet; she just needed to see how to bring it together.

Once you learn how to mix and match your wardrobe, you'll find infinite ways to reflect your authentic self. That same shift dress that Tracy wore could be styled a dozen different ways—whether your style leans edgy, boho, feminine, or punk rock. Not only can the same piece be styled to suit different personal styles, but it can also adapt to a wide range of occasions. Tracy's shift dress—once dismissed as too simple—could just as easily be dressed up for a formal work event or a job interview by pairing it with a sharp blazer and classic pumps. The same dress could be styled for a relaxed dinner out by adding a cozy scarf, a casual jacket, and a pair of riding boots. The key is learning how to combine your wardrobe pieces in ways to meet every occasion while expressing who you really are.

When you've taken the time to build a wardrobe that's tailored to your body, your coloring, your personality, and the realities of your lifestyle, creating outfits becomes easy. You have everything you need—pieces that flatter your shape, colors that harmonize naturally, and styles that feel authentically you. Whether you're rushing to a last-minute meeting or planning for a big event, you can quickly and effortlessly pull together the perfect look. Your wardrobe works for you with minimal effort, because it's built with intention. That gives you great control over your look—which can be incredibly exciting. Putting together outfits you love can then become an enjoyable, empowering experience—and even serve a type of self-care.

Ciara Dimou, a nurse practitioner and founder of VAIN Medi Spa, is a testament to this belief. A passionate advocate for women's empowerment, she champions the idea that everyone deserves self-love—and sees styling as a powerful way to express and nurture it.

A Testament to the Power of Styling: Ciara Dimou, AGNP-BC, WHNP-BC, Founder, VAIN Medi Spa

Cici encourages her patients to make themselves a priority and adapt the mindset that self-care isn't selfish—a message that really resonates with me. She believes that caring about how you present yourself leads to how you feel about yourself. It's about taking the time to show yourself the love you deserve.

I've been a nurse practitioner for ten years and am currently finishing up my doctorate. I've always focused on women's health and primary care. About eight years ago, I started working in the aesthetics space. I started VAIN Medi Spa out of my home. Now, I have a team of eight working out of a beautiful newly renovated space in Andover, Massachusetts.

At VAIN, we work hard to ensure that our patients feel they are in a safe environment to be heard, seen, and understood. In a business that can be inauthentic, it is important to us that we maintain authenticity. My desire to help women step out into the world feeling their best, as their authentic selves, is something Aricia and I really connected on. That's why I went into women's health to begin with.

I want to educate women that self-care isn't selfish, because when you're the best version of you, you're a better mom, a better friend, a better wife, a better sister—whatever it is. When you feel good about yourself, you are the best toward the people around you. And a big part of feeling good about yourself starts with feeling comfortable in how you are presenting yourself to the world.

First impressions are everything, and how you show up tells people how you want them to think of you. Style can help create that identity. Obviously, we have a lot of choice in what we put on our bodies, and it can be tough to navigate sometimes. I know that from my own work as well—people really value honest, fact-based guidance that will help them look their best while allowing their true self to shine.

I understand the challenges from my own experiences as well. As I've left my twenties behind, I've found that I tend to prioritize comfort more. I want something that both compliments me and that I'm comfortable in. Gone are the days where I would wear something just because it looked cute on the hanger, and I'd literally force it to fit! That approach leaves you feeling uncomfortable, and when you aren't comfortable, it can hurt your confidence.

In my conversations with Aricia, I've come to understand that it is possible to adapt your authentic style to whatever stage of life you're in. Whatever your age and whatever you're doing in life, giving some attention to what you wear is a powerful form of self-care that can be truly empowering when done right.

Essential Outfit Creation Concepts

When it comes to creating outfits, there are some foundational concepts that can elevate your outfits and bring a sense of balance, proportion, and intentionality to your looks. These are tools that can help you create polished, cohesive outfits with minimal effort. These are not rigid, but instead provide helpful guidelines to ensure that what you wear feels visually harmonious and thoughtfully put together.

Let's explore each of these concepts to understand how they can be used with outfit creation methods.

TRUST THE GOLDEN RATIO

The "Rule of Thirds" is a foundational concept from the visual arts that involves dividing an image into thirds to create a more dynamic and visually compelling composition. Since outfits are an essential form of visual expression, this principle can easily be applied to dressing. I like to think of it as the "Use of Thirds" when it comes to fashion. The goal is to divide your outfit, not your body, into three parts to create a 2:1 visual ratio that tends to make your look more interesting compared to dividing your outfit into equal halves. This ratio is actually a simplified version of the Golden Mean or Golden Ratio, and this approach brings more visual interest to your look by breaking it up in an intentional way.

As you're putting together outfits, focus on creating a visual break by pairing a longer and shorter garment. For example, wear high-waisted pants (which cover two-thirds) with a cropped jacket (one-third), or a long blouse with cropped pants. These breaks add dimension and balance to your look without any extra effort.

INCORPORATE ONLY ONE STATEMENT PIECE

The "One Statement Piece" approach is all about balance and focus in your outfit. It's a principle that encourages choosing a single bold or standout item to be the centerpiece of your look, allowing it to shine without overwhelming the overall outfit. Whether it's a vibrant scarf, an eye-catching pair of shoes, or a striking piece of jewelry, the idea is to let one Statement Piece take center stage while the rest of your outfit plays off of this main piece or remains neutral.

This not only makes the bold item more impactful but also leads to an overall more cohesive look. It gives your outfit a clear focal point, avoiding issues where various items are all competing for attention. This method helps simplify the process of building an outfit, as the Statement Piece can provide a clear direction for your choices or be used to top off a simple ensemble. You can effortlessly create a stylish and intentional look without overdoing it, making your entire ensemble feel curated and purposeful.

ADD A THIRD PIECE

The "Third Piece" concept is a simple yet powerful tool to instantly turn clothing into an outfit. The idea is that instead of relying on two basic pieces—like a top and bottom—adding a third element can bring depth, interest, and personality to your look. This Third Piece is often an extra layer or accessory, such as a blazer, jacket, scarf, or statement necklace, but it excludes shoes, which are considered a necessity. It's the finishing touch that makes an outfit feel intentional and complete.

Think of it this way: the first two pieces of your outfit form the foundation, while the Third Piece acts as the stylistic element that pulls everything together. It adds visual interest and can be a great way to express your personal style. I often share an example with clients that many of us can relate to: how a simple jeans-and-tee combo can instantly feel more put together with the addition of a tailored blazer or long cardigan or even just a necklace. Whether you're dressing for work, a casual day out, or an evening event, incorporating a Third Piece is an easy way to make your outfits feel more cohesive and refined, without overcomplicating things.

Level Up or Down as Needed

One of the most valuable qualities of a well-curated wardrobe is its ability to seamlessly transition outfits from casual to formal without needing to buy any new pieces. With today's fashion offering more flexibility than ever, this leveling approach allows you to adjust your outfits to suit the level of formality or casualness required for any situation by adapting the pieces in your wardrobe to multiple contexts. Whitney Torgerson, a stylist on our team, is a master of versatility, effortlessly creating outfits that transition across her diverse roles as a professional stylist and realtor and in her social life. She skillfully uses leveling to craft looks that suit every facet of her lifestyle.

Consider something as simple as a pair of black pants and a basic top. For a casual day at the office or working remotely, you might pair these pieces with comfortable flats and a slouchy cardigan. But if you need to step it up for an important meeting or formal event, you can easily elevate the same outfit by swapping the cardigan for a structured blazer, adding sleek heels, and accessorizing with understated jewelry. This simple shift takes your outfit from work casual to work formal without requiring a completely new outfit.

I like to think of this as "mixing your metaphors"—taking elements traditionally considered casual or relaxed and combining them with more formal pieces to find that perfect balance. A simple combination of jeans and a black T-shirt, for example, can be very casual when paired with sneakers and an oversized tote bag. On the other hand, it can be fancy enough for a night out when paired with an oversized pair of sparkling earrings and a small black clutch and heels.

To make the process of adjusting your outfits as easy as possible, I often recommend starting with one key piece that you need to wear or that best represents the level of dress you are aiming for. This might be an item dictated by a dress code, like a blazer, or a practical choice based on the weather, such as rain boots. Once you have your key piece, you can build the rest of the outfit around it, making incremental adjustments with each piece you add.

Now, as you assess your outfit, you can decide if you want to level it up or down. Rather than trying to make dramatic changes all at once, take a step-by-step approach. In general, the further apart the pieces you choose are in terms of formality, the more challenging it can be to make leveling work. For example, pairing a ball gown with sneakers requires a much finer touch to balance than, say, switching from sparkling heels to a more understated pair of heels with the same gown. The same idea applies to workwear. If you're trying to level down a formal blazer and black trousers, it's far easier to achieve a cohesive look with clean, dark jeans than with ripped denim, as the latter is much further down the dress scale. The more extreme the contrast, the trickier it can be to find the right balance.

The easiest way to start playing with leveling is to stay within close proximity in terms of dressiness and make more subtle adjustments. For instance, you might swap loafers for heels or a structured jacket for a cardigan. As you get more comfortable, you can push the boundaries a bit. Trends can also offer great inspiration—when suits with sneakers became popular, it was an example of more extreme leveling that worked because it was embraced on a wider scale. In the end, there are no strict rules, so don't be afraid to experiment and find combinations that feel right to you. The goal is to create a look that reflects your personal style while perfectly fitting the context.

On more than one occasion, I have spontaneously assisted a person in the restroom who showed up to an event overdressed. A few quick changes, like putting the sparkling statement necklace in the purse, toning down a bright-red lip, or folding up the shimmering shawl, can do wonders.

Next, we look at techniques and tools that can be used to elevate outfits—these can be used in combination with the outfit creation methods discussed in the subsequent section.

Strategies to Elevate Your Outfits

When I think about personal style, especially in the context of creating outfits, I see it as a spectrum. No matter your style—whether it leans classic, bold, or somewhere in between—your personal style is always evolving. If you're looking to enhance and refine that style, and move your outfits forward along this scale, this guide offers a series of actionable strategies to help you take your outfits to the next level.

Whether you feel like your look is missing something or you simply want to refine or elevate your style, these techniques are designed to empower you. They're adaptable to any style and work no matter where you are in your style journey. No matter if you're just starting out and feeling a bit hesitant—perhaps never having experimented with accessories, color, or prints—or you already have a bold and defined style, these strategies will help you enhance and evolve your style.

This list serves as an excellent reference when you glance in the mirror and feel that something is missing. If your outfit appears boring or lacks the excitement you envisioned, remember that you don't need to completely undress and start over. Often, a few subtle changes can transform your look.

With strategies such as adding a pop of color, layering clothes, and playing with proportions, you can elevate your outfit with minimal effort. This guide is your go-to resource for those final elements or details that can elevate your outfit, making it truly reflect your personal style.

ADD COLOR

One of the simplest ways to level up your outfit is by incorporating color. If your look is primarily composed of neutrals, consider introducing a non-neutral hue to create visual interest. For example, if you're wearing a black dress, adding a soft blue scarf adds interest, or adding a bright-red blazer can make a striking statement. If you are already wearing one non-neutral color but still feel your look lacks excitement, try adding a second analogous color—these are colors that sit next to each other on the color wheel, such as blue and green. Accessories like scarves, necklaces, bags, or shoes are easy ways to implement this idea, but you can also add color with any piece such as a top, bottom, or layer.

If you want to experiment further, consider wearing complementary colors, which are those located opposite each other on the color wheel. Pairing colors like blue and orange can create a bold effect, while mixing analogous colors, like purple and blue, brings a softer, more harmonious look.

PLAY WITH SCALE

You can also enhance an outfit by exaggerating the scale of pieces relative to your silhouette. The idea is to exaggerate and purposefully scale up a single element of your outfit to add interest and dimension to your look. For example, a hat with a brim three times wider than your head will naturally become a focal point—or consider the impact of a regular blazer versus a blazer with exaggerated shoulders. This approach isn't about following strict rules. Focus on how the element interacts with your look. Does it feel like a dominant feature? If so, it's likely doing its job to add visual interest and a sense of uniqueness to your style.

Large prints, an oversized ruffle, or chunky jewelry are all great ways to use scale to add boldness and personality to your look. Accessories offer a perfect opportunity to begin experimenting with scale. For instance, a skinny belt is going to be less dramatic than an oversized wide belt. Similarly, a necklace on a delicate gold chain is going to have a smaller, less exaggerated scale than a large statement necklace on a chunky chain, which will immediately add more interest. Earrings are yet another example. Consider the classic jeans and T-shirt outfit, and how it looks worn with plain stud earrings versus oversized hoops. By scaling up the earrings, the entire outfit is elevated.

Always remember, when you're adjusting scale—whether it's through accessories, prints, or layers—it should align with your Style ID. This ensures that the bolder elements you're incorporating fit seamlessly with your overall aesthetic and personal style.

ENHANCE WITH DETAILS

You can enhance your outfit by adding subtle details and points of interest. When clients think of outfit enhancements, most of my clients picture accessories like necklaces and earrings. But small touches like nail polish color can also make a big difference. For instance, bright-pink nails with gem accents create a much stronger impact than a barely there nude or pale pink. Similarly, a simple navy tee has less interest and personality than one with pink floral accents or a satin-trimmed neckline. Even layering two or three simple gold necklaces instead of one, or wearing a necklace, earrings, a ring, and a bracelet together, adds more style and detail to your outfit.

When I'm hosting styling events, I will often play a game where I have people tally up points for all the details and accessories they are wearing. It starts with how many colors they're wearing. Someone wearing one color gets one point, while someone wearing four colors gets four points. Then I ask how many pieces of clothing they're wearing. Say, if someone is wearing jeans and a T-shirt, that's two points. If they're wearing jeans, a T-shirt, and a jacket, that's three points. Nail polish can count as a point, as can glasses, etc. All these points add interest to an outfit and level it up—bringing depth and personality to your look.

INTRODUCE REPETITION OR FRICTION

Choose two or three key colors, patterns, or materials to repeat throughout your outfit to create a cohesive and dynamic appearance. For instance, if you wear a patterned scarf, incorporate that same pattern into your shoes or bag. Similarly, if you opt for a red top, choose red accessories—a bag, jewelry, and red shoes—to tie everything together seamlessly. Repetition is easy to implement and can have a big impact.

Friction involves mixing styles that might not traditionally go together, creating a unique and unexpected look. Though more nuanced to pull off, these unexpected combinations not only showcase your confidence but also infuse your outfit with an element of surprise, making it feel more personalized and unique. Consider pairing a tailored blazer with distressed jeans for an edgy yet polished vibe or combining a cargo pant with a silk blouse for a casual yet chic ensemble, or styling a lace or floral dress with combat boots to balance feminine and edgy elements. Experiment with different combinations that resonate with your style.

STYLE THOUGHTFULLY

Styling your outfit goes beyond simply putting on clothes; it's about making each piece feel truly your own. It's not just *what* you wear but *how* you wear it that helps define your style. Experiment with different tucking styles, such as fully tucked, half-tucked, or untucked, to transform the look and feel of an outfit. Cuffing the sleeves of your blazer, popping the collar of your shirt, or unbuttoning a few buttons can enhance your outfit by bringing more personality and polish to your whole look.

Amy Finegold, a stylist on my team, is a great example. She doesn't wear much color herself, but she's a master at working with neutrals, mixing textures and structured pieces, and using styling techniques like cuffing jeans and layering. Her outfits are always polished, impressive, and completely her! We all have our own preferences, so it's perfectly fine to choose among these methods to find a way to add depth and interest in a way that works with your Style ID. The key is creating looks you love that feel authentically you.

Putting Together Outfits

Once you have a wardrobe based on your Style ID, putting together outfits becomes much easier. With a systematic approach, you can easily create outfits that range from casual to glam, depending on what your day holds. Are you running errands and want to be comfortable? Or running errands and hoping to bump into your crush? Are you going out for lunch with clients and want to be polished and professional? Or lunching with the girls and want to turn on the glam? Whether you're headed to a business lunch or a relaxed afternoon with friends, knowing how to build the right outfit ensures you're always prepared.

As you try different approaches to outfit creation, you may find that you prefer one method over another. Or you may find that you want to alter your approach according to the day, the occasion, or even the mood. You can use whichever technique makes you the most comfortable. Regardless of how you approach it, the first step before building any outfit is to step back and consider your day. True style is about being comfortable and confident in an outfit that not only works for the situation but also reflects your authentic personal style. Therefore, you want to head into your closet with basic practicalities in mind like:

1. **Where am I going?** Consider what activities you're going to be participating in for most of your time, wherever you're headed. Are you going to be walking a lot? Driving? Standing? Sitting? These considerations will help guide decisions on footwear, layering, and the overall functionality of your outfit.

2. **How's the weather?** Is it pouring rain outside? Is there snow and ice on the ground? Or maybe it's scorching hot and humid—will you need to worry about sweating through your outfit? How about layers if you are moving between hot outdoors and chilly air-conditioned spaces? Dressing appropriately for the weather ensures your outfit not only stays looking great but also functions well throughout the day.

3. **What's the level of dress?** Deciding how dressed up or down you want to be sets the tone for your entire look. In today's more casual world, this question has become even more

relevant. If we are unsure how we want to show up on a given day, it's nearly impossible to create that perfect outfit that makes us feel confident and comfortable. Taking a moment to consider this can save a considerable amount of time. You can easily level an outfit up or down the spectrum from casual to formal, but you want to avoid starting too far off the mark. Also consider any relevant dress codes. While many environments have relaxed their rules, there are still occasions where certain dress standards, explicit or implicit, are a consideration.

Any one of the questions above or a combination can have a big impact on how you build an outfit. For example, if you need to wear a rain boot and need to be more business formal, you can level up your outfit with other pieces like a blazer since you cannot wear a more formal business shoe. With these questions answered, you are ready to explore outfit creation methods.

IMPLEMENT AN OUTFIT FORMULA

One of the easiest ways to put together outfits is using outfit formulas. An outfit formula is a specific combination of pieces that you can wear in a lot of different versions. It is similar to having a set uniform, like some entrepreneurs that wear a black tee and jeans and black lace-ups every day, but with more flexibility. With an outfit formula, you can achieve the same simplicity with more variation. It could be that you always pair skinny jeans with a shell, blazer, and sneakers, but keep a range of colors and styles for each piece. When combined, these elements create distinctly different looks, even though you're using the same four foundational pieces. A lot of people do this naturally. Maybe you already have a formula or two that you use.

Once you identify your favorite formulas, you can easily expand them by adding new pieces within the same categories. Part of my personal uniform is a set of basic tank tops from Target that I love. I have five tank tops in different colors, all in my palette: gray, blue, and off-white. Some have a V-neck and some a high neck. I pair them with my blue or black wide-leg denim and one of my three pairs of sneakers. In this example, if I start with blue and black wide-leg jeans paired with five different tanks, adding gray jeans and another tank expands my options to three pairs of jeans, six tanks, and three sneakers—resulting in fifty-four possible combinations. Having fifty-four options provides a highly efficient way to build outfits and expand your wardrobe with combinations you already know you love.

You can also easily expand your formula by adding an item. For example, I like to add a casual, loose-fitting blazer to this formula. It's formal enough for a video call for work but still comfortable and not overly stuffy. With my 2 blazers, I now have 3 pairs of jeans, 6 tanks, 3 sneakers, and 2 blazers, adding up to 108 combinations!

If you already have a favorite formula, like the one above, you can expand your options even further by combining it with a second formula. Let's say your second formula is a classic button-up shirt plus wide-leg trousers plus loafers. By mixing pieces from both formulas, you can create a wide range of new looks. For instance, you could pair one of the tank tops with the wide-leg trousers and add loafers for a business-casual outfit. Or try combining the button-up shirt with jeans and sneakers from the first formula for a polished yet relaxed look. Mixing across formulas like this allows you to create fresh combinations with pieces you already have, giving you even more variety and options.

The enhancement strategies we listed earlier are also an excellent way to dramatically increase your outfit options—adding a simple accessory, layer, or pop of color can transform each combination, giving you even more versatility and interest within your formulas.

One Outfit Formula of Ten Pieces

5 Tanks

2 Wide Leg Jeans

3 Sneakers

5 x 2 x 3 = 30 Outfits

The many different looks you can achieve with just 10 pieces

To create your own outfit formulas, start by thinking about what outfit formulas you may already be implementing. Is there an outfit you wear over and over again, or a variation of it? It's probably something you feel comfortable and confident in—something you know works for you and that you enjoy wearing. Identifying why it works for you and why you like it can then help you create other outfit formulas, expanding your repertoire. Check your mood board and see if there are outfit formulas that stand out that you have not tried yet. Once you identify your favorite formulas, you can easily and efficiently expand them by bringing in additional pieces that fit your formula.

Next, we will look at some step-by-step methods for building an outfit.

BUILD AN OUTFIT OFF OF BASICS

This is the most straightforward method, and the one I use whenever I am in a rush. First you create your base by choosing basics for your top and bottom in neutrals. Basics are those go-to items that are clean and neutral (black, beige, gray, navy, white), allowing them to pair easily—they could be your ID essentials or other basics you own.

The base can consist of a top and bottom or, for example, a dress. As you add the next pieces, start with the necessary first, like shoes or a belt. As you do so, consider our list of tools used to enhance an outfit and go ahead and mix different colors of neutrals, add textures, and play with different styling like rolling the sleeves. Continue to add more go-to basic items in neutrals to make your outfit complete—a layer, a bag, or a simple necklace. As I tell my clients, jeans and a T-shirt is just jeans and a T-shirt, but jeans, a T-shirt, and a necklace is an outfit.

The next level of building off of basics again starts with your neutral base, but here we introduce one Statement Piece to "make" the look, while keeping everything else—shoes, bag, and other items—

simple and neutral. A single statement is all you need to complete a cohesive, elevated look built of basics.

Another approach to building off basics is to again create your neutral base, and then incorporate pieces that add interest without being bold Statement Pieces. Instead, incorporate subtle yet intriguing accessories or a mix of accessories that have interest—a silk scarf, a colored or textured shoe, or unique jewelry. These additions can bring a touch of color or stay within a neutral palette, adding depth and personality to your outfit.

CREATE AN OUTFIT WITH COLOR

There are several different ways to build outfits with color as the foundation, and it's easy when you have your palette for reference. Wearing all one color often lacks contrast and therefore interest—so if you prefer all black, for example, bring in texture and sheen to add interest. Wearing all one color in non-neutrals, say red, has a sense of drama, but texture can still break up the color and add interest.

Neutrals are incredibly versatile and can be mixed and matched effortlessly without clashing, making them a great tool for building any outfit. They work together harmoniously, allowing for endless combinations that always look cohesive and polished, making them a go-to choice for creating balanced outfits with minimal effort. Keep it simple and choose a dark and a light neutral from your palette to start, like cream and charcoal, and add other neutral pieces and accessories without worry. Reference your list of tools to enhance an outfit, and consider textures, styling, and structure too.

The next level of creating an outfit with color is to start with one non-neutral piece paired with neutrals. For example, if you have a burgundy jacket, pair it with black pants and a gray or cream top, keeping the rest of the outfit—like shoes and jewelry—in neutral tones, such as black shoes and gold accessories. Many people find it easier to build an outfit from neutrals and then add a single pop of color. This approach works well since neutrals naturally complement any single color, making it easy to avoid clashing.

If you want to take it further, introduce a second color. For instance, you could add a complementary shade like forest green, or an analogous hue like rich purple, along with your original color and neutrals. This lets you build a layered, cohesive look with added interest and depth.

START WITH A STATEMENT PIECE

When building an outfit around a bold Statement Piece, start by considering what makes it unique and eye-catching. Maybe it has an oversized silhouette, an unexpected texture, or an intense color. The Statement Piece could have a distinct style, like a Victorian necklace or a futuristic metallic top. By identifying these standout characteristics, you can decide how to enhance or balance them to create a cohesive look.

One option is to lean into the style of your Statement Piece by choosing complementary items that echo its features. For instance, if your Statement Piece is a vibrant red jacket, you could pair it with red shoes or a red belt, creating a coordinated and bold look. Or if you have a textured piece, like a sequined top, consider subtle textures in other items—such as a silky scarf or patent leather bag. This approach works well if you're aiming for a bold, head-turning outfit that amplifies the personality of your Statement Piece.

Alternatively, you can create balance by pairing the Statement Piece with items that contrast its style, adding intrigue and depth. A Victorian necklace might pair beautifully with a sleek blazer, or a graphic tee can be balanced with neutral trousers and simple loafers.

This approach allows the Statement Piece to shine while keeping the outfit grounded, and it's perfect if you prefer a more subtle yet sophisticated look.

An Outfit Flowchart: The Ultimate Guide

This is the most comprehensive method for creating an outfit, built to help walk you through any scenario and help you get unstuck if you are struggling. This step-by-step guide provides an overall method and order for creating an outfit.

Begin by selecting one item that either inspires you or is essential for your day. This could be a practical item like shoes or pants, depending on the activities ahead. For example, if you'll be walking a lot, comfortable shoes are a must, but if you're attending a meeting, you may want to prioritize a sharp look. Alternatively, you can start with an inspirational item, such as a new top you're excited to wear or a bold accessory like a scarf. This inspirational piece will set the tone for the rest of the outfit.

THE STYLE FORMULA

How to Make an Outfit:

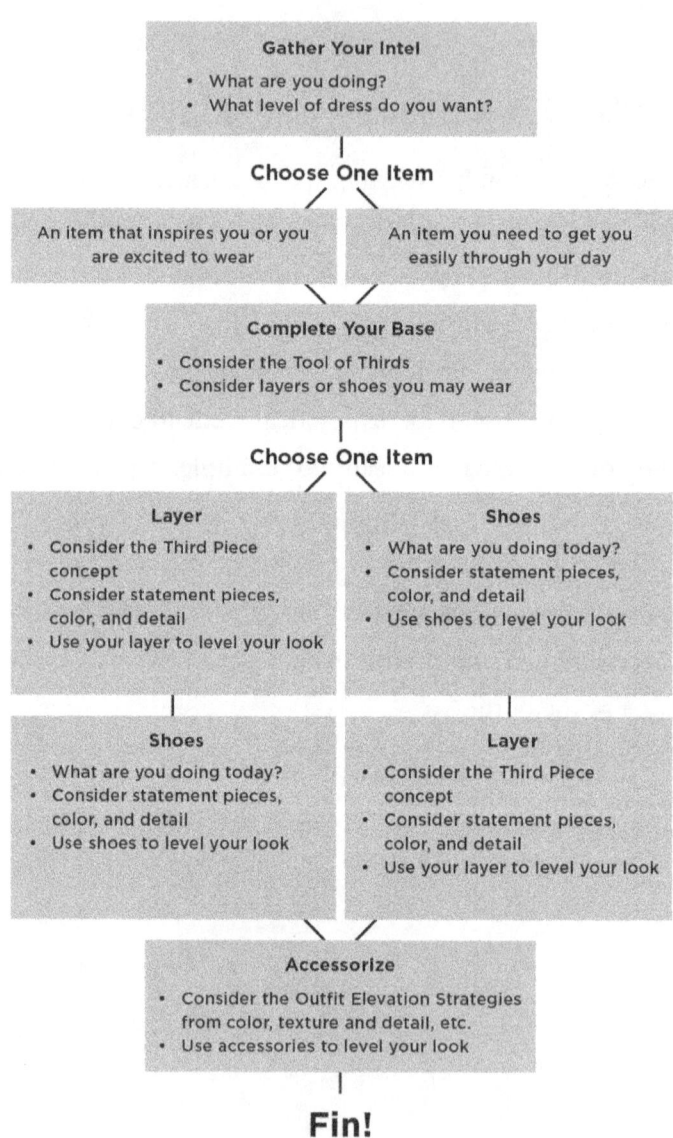

Your own outfit creation flowchart

Next, you want to build your base, choosing a top and bottom or single piece that relates to your first piece. Keep the 2:1 ratio in mind and opt for complementary silhouettes: if one piece is loose, balance it with something more fitted.

Then, add your shoes and a layer, considering the Third Piece concept. With each piece you add, check your level of casual to formal so you can adjust as you build your outfit. For example, shoes can dramatically shift the feel of an outfit and are great for leveling an outfit up or down in formality. Sneakers can make a dressier look more casual, while heels or formal shoes can elevate jeans. A layer, such as a jacket or cardigan, can also level up or down. A blazer adds structure and formality, while a jean jacket or cardigan brings a relaxed, casual vibe. If you choose to skip the layer, simply add more interest by moving to the next step where we add accessories.

Now, we add accessories to complete your look. Accessories can take an outfit to new heights, adding sophistication, fun, or personality. If you haven't chosen a focal point, now is the time to do so. Try a Statement Piece—perhaps a necklace or belt—or layer smaller accessories together for a bolder impact. Use accessories to highlight an area of your body or add dimension to a simpler outfit. Mixing textures, colors, and styles can add interest, as long as there's a unifying element.

Lastly, make any final adjustments. Look at your outfit as a whole. Does it feel too formal or too casual? Make small adjustments using the leveling techniques like switching shoes or adding or removing accessories. Check that the outfit has enough interest through colors, textures, or layers. This approach to outfit creation is designed to give you flexibility, making it easy to adjust your look while keeping things simple and efficient—so you can step out in style with minimal fuss.

A Style Formula for Success

All my clients share one thing: a desire to look great without great effort. The Style Formula gives them—and you—the tools to rely on to make that possible for any occasion. By defining your unique Style ID, this formula simplifies the entire process of getting dressed, guiding you in creating outfits that make you feel your best. Outfits that reflect your personal preferences in everything from your body architecture to your authentic personal style. Outfits you feel good in. Outfits that work for your day-to-day life, whatever that may look like.

The more you put these ideas into practice, the easier—and the more fun—it will be. You will have the ability to explore the creative side of styling for yourself, knowing you have the tools of your Style ID to guide you. And that is how you will further develop that authentic style, reflecting it in every outfit you put together. It starts with the science, then you unlock the art. You will then master the Style Formula—the art and science of what to wear.

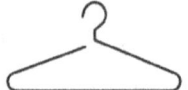

To the Closet: Create Your Portfolio

Professional stylists will usually have a portfolio of work that they use to showcase what they do, comprised of photos of people they have styled in outfits put together by the stylist. Every client I work with receives a portfolio of outfits they can refer to, and now, I want you to do the same for yourself. Create an image folder online or an album on your phone—somewhere easy to access—where you can store your outfit photos. It will serve as a quick reference whenever you need inspiration and allow you to seamlessly add new looks as you create them.

Experiment with the techniques outlined in this chapter and put together some new outfits. Whenever you create one you love, take a photo of yourself in it—this is the start of your portfolio. You can even organize the photos into categories or add searchable notes for easy reference. As you continue implementing what you have learned, keep adding to your collection by photographing each outfit that makes you feel great.

Your portfolio will benefit you in a few ways. First, it's a great exercise in fine-tuning the styling skill you've learned, and seeing what works and what doesn't, and in identifying patterns as far as what you do and do not like. Second, it's a convenient reference point for those moments of "What do I wear?" Wear the same outfit again or use a favorite outfit formula and swap out one piece for another. Unfoldid's online master class has an area where you can upload photos and categorize them, for instance, so you can quickly reference outfits for designated occasions, from work to travel.

I often snap a photo of myself when I'm headed out the door in an outfit I like. I have a whole collection, and whenever I'm not sure what to wear, I can flip through and look at outfits I've already created for myself and pick one that fits the moment. It's convenient for traveling as well, allowing me to quickly pick and pack complete outfits I love.

In this way, your styling portfolio becomes much like a recipe book. There are probably recipes you love to make in summer, when it's hot out, like a refreshing salad. Other recipes, like hearty soups, fit better to a chilly winter day. Once you start to categorize your outfits photographically, you will have a "recipe" for every occasion.

Unlock more style insights! Scan the QR code for exclusive content and interactive exercises to deepen your understanding of the chapter's key concepts and help you further explore your Style ID.

CONCLUSION

"When did you get so stylish?"

The question was posed to me at a family dinner sometime in my thirties by one of my brothers. They had grown up with me running around in muddy work boots, ripped jeans, and oversized T-shirts. Seeing their little sister show up at Thanksgiving dinner in carefully tailored trousers and a feminine dusky-rose blouse was a surprise. And the answer to their question was simple: "I learned it."

Just like cooking, carpentry, or coding, styling is a skill we can all learn. I learned it. I've had thousands of clients learn it. And you can learn it too. This book covers the essentials of the Style Formula. By learning about your body architecture, color palette, fashion likes, and lifestyle, as well as methods to build a wardrobe and create outfits, you have gained an understanding of the components that make up your Style ID. The most exciting part is still ahead—bringing your unique style to life. You've read the textbook; now it's time to show off what you know.

This is a journey, not a makeover. The traditional idea of a makeover usually means making such a drastic change that the authentic essence of the person is lost in the process, and that's not the goal here. Unlocking your Style ID is about revealing and celebrating who you are, bringing your authentic self to the surface.

Take my own style journey. I shared that, as a child, I rebelled against all things I perceived as "girly"—frills, lace, ruffles, and, above all, the color pink. I refused to wear it. That stuck with me well into my thirties. Then, a new color trend took hold. Colors, like all other things in fashion, come in and out of vogue. And that season, a sort of dusky-rose hue was *the* color to wear. By this time, I was working as a stylist, and when I saw that particular shade, something unexpected happened. I thought, "Hm, that's actually in my color palette … and I'm so drawn to it!" I gave it a shot—and loved it. That dusky rose has since become a staple in my wardrobe, and I now have several favorite pieces in that very color.

Although eight-year-old me could never have imagined wearing pink of any kind, my grown-up style has stayed true to the "tomboy" style of my childhood. I still avoid frills and ruffles and lace, preferring structured, sharp silhouettes and clean lines. By using the Style Formula, I have found a way to dress that is true to who I am at my core—still that little girl mucking around on the farm—but in a way that fits my current life. And it feels very good.

I want you to capture that feeling of *very good* too. I want you to feel comfortable in your clothes. Not only that but empowered. In control. My hope for you is that your wardrobe becomes a source of confidence and ease. That you step out each day knowing your clothes don't just fit your life—they celebrate who you are. Now that you have a firm understanding of yourself and a knowledge of how clothing can work for you, you have the tools you need to make it happen.

And what makes this truly exciting is that we have more freedom in how we dress than ever before. In the second chapter, we looked at some of those old norms and even laws, like women being banned from wearing pants. That is in the past. Now, we are living in a time when nonbinary fashion graces magazine covers, and rigid office dress codes are becoming a thing of the past. We all have so much more choice. Everyone can wear everything. That's incredibly liberating.

What you wear will evolve as you evolve, going through the various wonderful phases and stages of life. The great thing is, your Style ID will always be there for you. It's your reliable, honest best friend, right there in the closet with you, helping you avoid fashion crises and wardrobe frustrations. With your Style ID as your guide, you'll be able to navigate each new chapter feeling confident, empowered, and truly yourself.

You are on the way to dressing with ease and confidence. And if you want help on your journey, I am here for you. My website is full of helpful resources, from checklists to how-to guides, and even an online master class in your Style ID to expand your styling know-how. And, of course, you can always book time with me or one of the Unfoldid stylists. We are here to make the journey enjoyable and to share in that moment of joy when you say, "I got this." And we're ready to do a happy dance with you in your closet when you discover *your* unique Style ID!

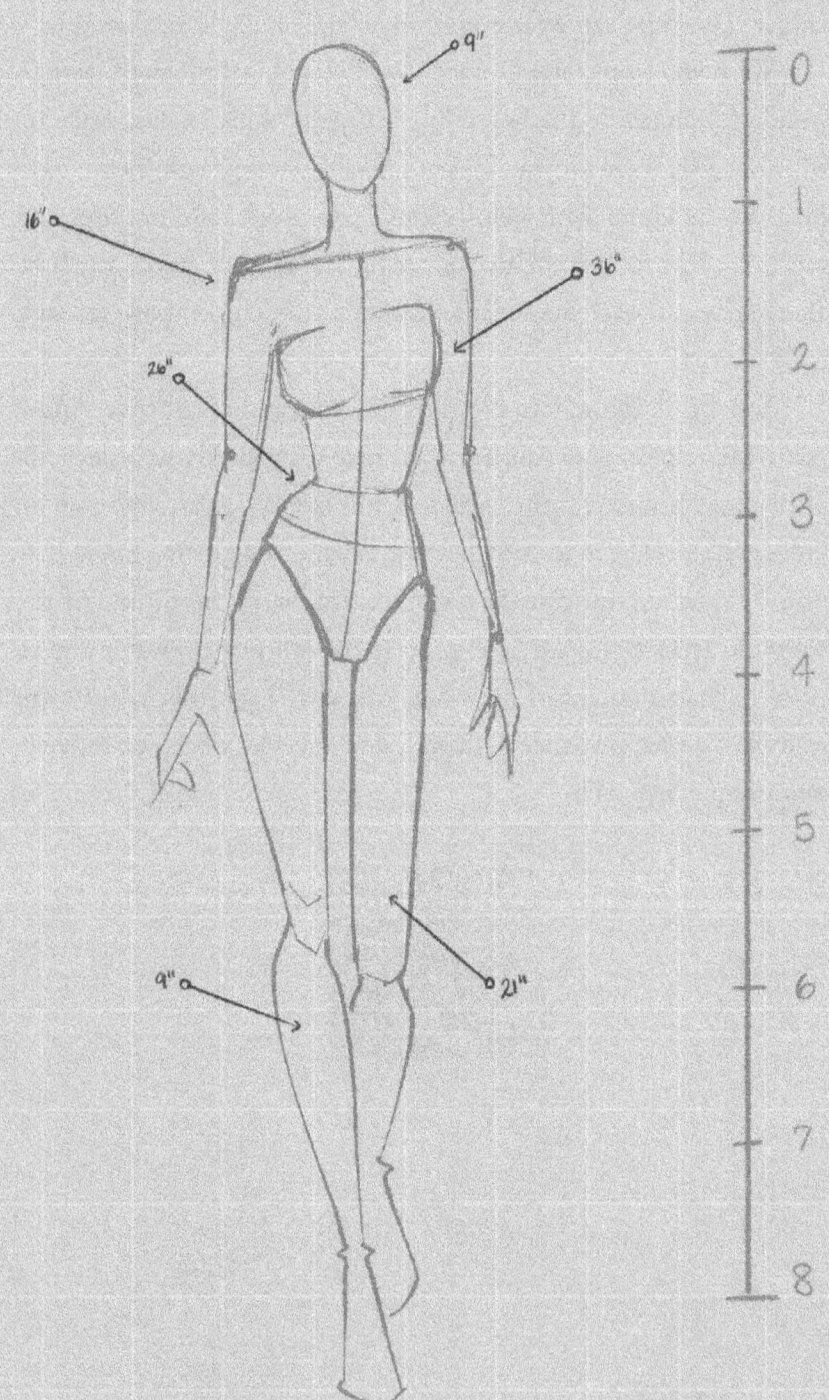

ACKNOWLEDGMENTS

To Rani Wise for taking this journey with me.

To the Unfoldid team, your expertise and creativity inspire me and our clients every day.

To my clients, who have generously shared their style journeys with me for so many seasons.

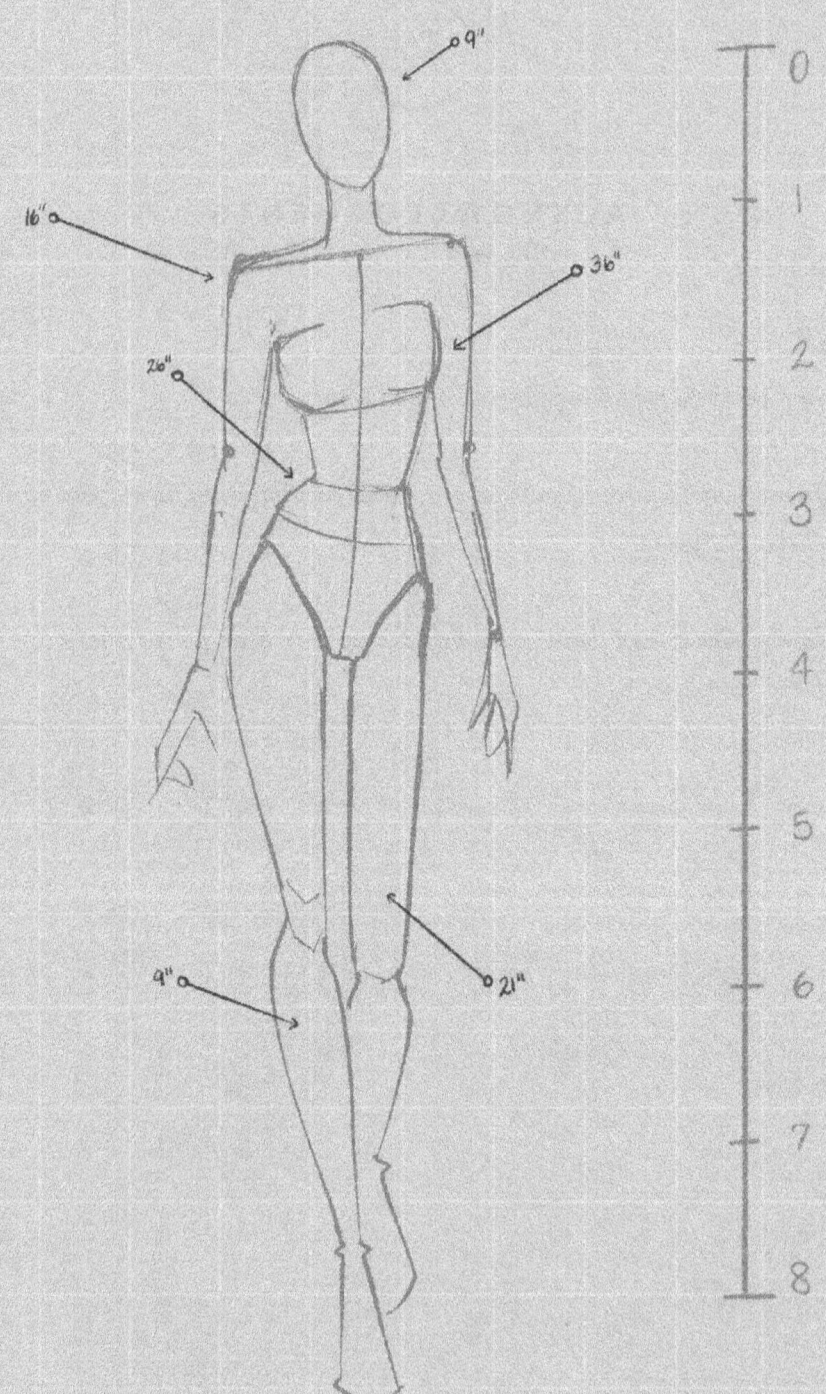

ABOUT THE AUTHOR

Aricia Symes was born in New England as the only girl of five kids. As a child, she was a self-proclaimed tomboy, mucking around on her family's farm in overalls and work boots and roughhousing with her brothers. Today, she's the founder and master stylist of Unfoldid, a personal styling company that prioritizes personal wellbeing. When people ask her, "How did you get to be so stylish?!" she tells them: "I learned it." Aricia believes that anyone can learn the foundations of style and has dedicated her career to helping people from all walks of life master the art and science of style.

Before founding Unfoldid in 2010, Aricia got her foot in the door of the fashion industry working for an international shoe company in Asia. She maintained a focus on fashion while employed as a consultant for Ernst & Young in Vienna, Austria. Her international experiences continue to inform her work as a stylist today. Ultimately, her love of fashion motivated her to get into styling, a field where she could work closely with people, exercise her creativity, and balance her family life. She learned the ins and outs of styling and coloring from established experts in the field, like Paula Slattery and Stacy London. Using what she'd learned, she developed the objective elements of her own Style Formula, a tool people can use to identify their Style Identity—or Style ID.

Today, Aricia has finetuned that Style Formula to a science, which she teaches not only to individual clients but also to larger groups through speaking engagements and courses. With this book, she brings her teachings to a wider audience, encouraging all of her readers to unfold their Style ID.

Aricia holds a double degree in International Business and Asian Studies from the University of Vermont and an MBA from the Stern School of Business at New York University. She currently lives in the Boston area with her husband, three children, and dog.